Contents

CONVERSION TABLE – metric to imperial

millilitres to fluid ounces	multiply by 0.035	ie 30ml=1 fl oz 20ml=0.7 fl oz
grams to ounces	multiply by 0.03527	ie 7g=0.25oz
kilograms to pounds	multiply by 2.205	ie 1kg=2.2lbs 18kg=40lbs
°C to °F	multiply by 9/5 & add 32	ie 65°C=150°F 60°C=140°F

About the Authors

David Gee and Matthew Gee
In 2000 brothers David and Matthew became partners in a coffee wholesaler/specialty roaster based in Sydney's Artarmon. After learning how to blend and roast coffee, the brothers went on to purchase four up-market cafés in Brisbane called GOSH Coffee and operated them for five years.

David and Matthew have since moved on from café ownership and their original wholesaler/specialty roaster and after branching out on their own and later consulting for a large Melbourne-based coffee company, they decided to concentrate full time on their coffee training business. Their Barista Basics™ Coffee Academy, a purpose-built café for this instruction was completed in mid-2003 and relocated in 2005 and again in 2008. The Barista Basics™ course itself is the result of two years of research involving university trained teachers, professional baristas and industry leaders. It is undoubtedly the most well-regarded course of its type in Australia and is the only barista school in Australia to carry TAFE affiliation. David and Matthew are widely regarded in the coffee industry as Australia's leading barista trainers.

Matthew and David have been feature writers for industry magazines Bean Scene and Tea and Coffee Asia. They have appeared on Australian television on Bert Newton's *Good Morning Australia*, Channel 9's *Fresh* with Jeff Jansz, NBN's *Today Extra* with Nat Jeffery and have made several appearances on Channel 9's *Mornings with Kerri-Anne*. Their most recent appearance as this edition went to print was a feature segment on Channel 9's *A Current Affair*. They have worked as official espresso tasters for *Choice Magazine's* 2004-2010 reviews of home espresso machines. David and Matthew created the world's first coffee art class in 2004. Their coffee art was recently featured in a two-page colour spread in London's Daily Mail newspaper and also a print and TV ad campaign for a major coffee brand.

Since 2008 Barista Basics™ Coffee Academy has been a registered training organisation (RTO) offering nationally accredited courses. It is also the only coffee school in Australia to be TAFE accredited.

David Gee - background
David has a Bachelor of Commerce, from the University of New South Wales, Australia and an MBA from the William E. Simon Business School at the University of Rochester, New York, USA.

He started his working life as an accountant and a stockbroker, before moving into the entertainment industry, working in licensing and promotions for The Walt Disney Company in Hong Kong and Melbourne from 1992-1996 and then in his own licensing company with his two brothers, Andrew and Matthew. This company operated across eight Asian countries and saw David living in Singapore from 1996-2000.

Matthew Gee - background
Matthew has a Bachelor of Economics (Honours) degree and a Bachelor of Laws (Honours) degree, both from the University of Sydney, Australia. From 1994-95 he was a tutor and workshop lecturer at the University of Sydney's Accounting Faculty whilst completing his degree. Matthew lived in Singapore from 1996-2000, co-running the Gee brothers' Wave Licensing International.

In 1999 David and Matthew started Wave Entertainment Pty Limited in Australia which specialises in producing high quality children's television programs. Their first creation of 26 x half hour pre-school shows entitled Zirkos Kids, has aired in over 18 countries.

One of our cafés

David Gee and Matthew Gee

The History of the Bean

Goats, Monasteries and Penny Universities

Yemen has long taken all the kudos for "inventing" coffee (indeed it has even been validated by being the correct answer on the television show 'Who Wants To Be A Millionaire' – if Ian 'Molly' Meldrum only knew the answer he would have won $1,000,000 for charity rather than $500,000!). As American coffee-guru Kenneth Davids points out[1] however, here is significant botanical evidence to indicate that arabica coffee originated on the plateaus of central Ethiopia. There it grew wild, over a thousand metres above sea level. To this day, it still does, as well as in other regions on the African continent including Cameroon, Ivory Coast, Uganda, Angola and Zaire.

Whether or not the Ethiopians introduced the coffee tree to Yemen during their successful invasion of southern Arabia in AD525 is uncertain, but the Yemen is acknowledged as the first place in the world that coffee was *cultivated* from the sixth century onwards.

The most popular story about the beginnings of coffee centres around an A.D.800 goat herder from Yemen by the name of Kaldi, who noticed his goats becoming alarmingly frisky after munching on some berries from a coffee tree. He also decided to taste some and became immediately invigorated. He took a sample of the berries to a local monastery and told his story to the Imam, who subjected the berries to a series of scientific tests. The first was to dry the berry, then boil it and drink the resulting liquid. From then on, neither the Imam nor his followers ever nodded off again at worship sessions and the drink became the drink of choice across monasteries throughout Arabia.

The world's first coffee shop opened in Constantinople in 1475 and by late that century, coffee was a favourite drink of the

---

[1] Davids, K. (2001) *Coffee: A Guide to Buying, Brewing and Enjoying.* New York: St Martin's Griffin, p 11

Arabs. Although they tried to stop people from taking fertile seeds out of the country they failed miserably and whilst coffee would not grow in Europe (it cannot tolerate frost), it did take in places like India, Indonesia, Haiti, Mexico, the Caribbean and South America.

The Europeans have been enjoying coffee since the early 1600s. The now spiritual home of coffee, Italy had its first coffeehouse open its doors in 1654. By the late 1600s coffee had reached the American colonies. At the turn of the century it was an entrenched drink across the civilised world and coffeehouses became the new meeting places for the educated and elite.

In England, coffee houses were called 'penny universities' (a penny was charged for admission and a cup of coffee). The word 'TIPS' was reputedly coined in an English coffeehouse. A sign reading 'To Insure Prompt Service' (TIPS) was placed by a cup. Those desiring prompt service and better seating threw a coin into a tin.

At this time coffee was made in the Turkish style - ground to a powder, sweetened (usually), boiled and filtered through a fabric strainer to remove the bulkier sediment.

The Origins of the Espresso Machine[2]
The first real breakthrough in the tinkering with pressure, steam, gaskets and chambers to create espresso came in 1901 when Luigi Bezzera patented a steam pressure machine that distributed the coffee through groups directly into the cup. Dessiderio Pavoni purchased the patent in 1903 and manufactured machines based on the Bezzera machine and others soon followed.

In the 1940s, a barista from Milan named Gaggia, developed an intricate machine involving pistons that was able to produce a higher pressure than previous machines. The new 'lever group' machine could force water through an even more tightly packed

---

[2] for a more detailed history of the espresso machine, see Davids, K. (1993) *Espresso: Ultimate Coffee.* California: 101 Productions/Cole Group, chapter 2

bed of coffee and at much greater pressure than ever before, ensuring the full extraction that we are familiar with today. Gaggia noticed an oily substance on the top of the espresso and instead of this being a liability ("What was that scum on the top of the coffee?" engineers would ask) Gaggia turned it into an asset and marketed the machine as being able to produce coffee *so rich that the coffee produced its very own cream.* 'Crema Caffe/Naturale' became synonymous with good coffee. Today, this 'crema' is recognised as the mark of a properly extracted espresso.

The Cimbali and Faema machines that followed in the 50s and 60s further revolutionised the espresso machine industry. These *semi-automatic* machines, where espresso poured out in pre-set volumes, meant that whilst baristas still had to load the groups, press a button, tip out the spent coffee and froth the milk, the espresso they created was much more consistent than ever before, and much easier to make. We own one of Australia's oldest fully restored Faema machines. It is a 1956 lever model and is so good looking that we are reluctant to use it even though the espresso that it produces is pure gold.

Pride of place in our Sydney training room is this restored 1956 Faema Urania

Now, even established gourmet coffee outlets such as Starbucks are using *fully automatic* machines that do everything from grinding beans to pouring espressos, frothing milk and

8

delivering the same cup every time, at the push of a button. These machines are expensive (over $20,000) but can they ever replace the true barista who prepares the espresso and froths the milk so that it becomes creamy, silky and creamy? Probably not. Not yet anyway.

For those who are interested, we've written an article on the history of espresso in Australia that can be found on our website www.baristabasics.com.au in the articles section.

This oldie is still working in a café at Kempsey, NSW

The modern espresso machine

Growing, Roasting and Blending Coffee

Types of Coffee
Botanists will tell you that there are over 6,000 species of coffee plant with at least 25 major types. So let's cut to the chase. The two most important varieties that we need to know about are arabica (pronounced a-ra-bi-kah) and robusta (pronounced row-bust-ah).

Arabica
The good stuff, the expensive stuff and the stuff roasters most often boast about, arabica coffee is the best tasting coffee. It is grown on trees, usually at high altitudes and has a superior taste to robusta. However, because arabica coffee is very prone to frost, pests (coffee-bean borer and coffee-leaf miner) and disease (spore-forming fungus), its yield is lower than robusta and it is harder to grow.

When roasters boast that their blend is "100% arabica" they mean that to be a good thing, as arabica coffee is universally considered to have a much smoother taste than robusta. The bean itself looks fairly similar to a robusta bean, but it is larger, harder and more dense. The fruit is oval.

Regions growing arabica coffee include South America, Africa, India and Indonesia. 60% of the world's coffee comes from arabica coffee trees.

They grow to 5-7 metres (16-23ft), but are usually pruned to 2-3 metres (6.5-10ft) to aid in the picking process, which is still to this day, mainly done by hand.

Each tree can produce between 0.5kg-5.5kg (1.1-12lbs) of green beans per year. It takes 5kg (11lbs) of cherries to produce 1kg (2.2lbs) of beans.

When planted from seed, the arabica tree usually takes about three years to bear fruit, and six years to mature. The tree will usually produce a good crop for up to about fifteen years. It will then be pruned to about 30cm (1ft) above the ground and the strongest two sprouts of the stump are then permitted to mature.

About two hours per day of direct sunlight is ideal for the arabica tree.

Each arabica cherry usually contains two green beans, whose flat sides sit together. Arabica trees like well watered, but well drained soil, no frost but also no hot extremes.

They are planted between 3-4 metres (10-13ft) apart.

Robusta

The poor cousin of the arabica is the robusta. Robusta grows on a shrub, is usually not grown at altitude and has a higher caffeine content than the arabica bean. Robusta coffee is more resilient than arabica and its yield higher but unfortunately it is considered by many to be inferior in taste to the arabica, at least on its own.

Close to 40% of the world's coffee comes from robusta coffee trees.

First discovered in the Congo, robusta grows in West and Central Africa, Vietnam, India and in small parts of South America.

When planted from seed, the robusta tree usually takes about two years to bear fruit.

The fruit is round but the seeds are oval in shape and smaller than their arabica counterparts.

Italian blends have always had a fair amount of robusta in them (sometimes up to 40%) but roasters in places like Australia, New Zealand, the United States of America and Canada are only now discovering the merits of high grade robusta (Indian robusta is a good example). Used in small quantities in blends, robusta acts to improve the depth of quality and crema thickness of the espresso.

Telling if Your Blend has Robusta in it

As a broad rule of thumb, when placed crack down on a bench, robsuta beans will roll over. When arabica beans are placed crack down they will generally not roll over as they are flatter on one side than robustas which are generally round. Robustas look more like ball bearings, arabicas more like peanuts.

Harvesting Coffee

Not many people know this, but green coffee beans come from oval-shaped cherries. The cherries look a little like grapes or olives. Once the jasmine-like white flowers at the extremities of the coffee tree have fallen to the ground, the cherries form as clusters at the base of the leaves. They take about six months to mature. On any given tree you might find both green and red cherries. The red ones are the ripe ones and have to be picked before they shrivel up and become raisin-like.

To this day, the cherries are still largely hand-picked for a couple of key reasons. Firstly, in most coffee-growing countries labour is cheap so there is no economic incentive to use machinery. Secondly, the terrain of the land in these countries often prohibits machinery to work effectively.

Harvest time is a busy time on coffee plantations with scores of brightly-dressed pickers with large metal buckets making their way down the rows of trees.

Recently we visited a coffee grower outside Ballina on the NSW North Coast (close to Byron Bay). This grower still uses manual labour at harvest time to pick the cherries (although he is testing machines this year). He maintains that most Australian growers do the same. There are certainly machines employed in Australia, Brazil and Hawaii which shake the tree just vigorously enough to displace the ripe cherries but this method has proven to be nowhere near as effective as the hand-picking method. It is however a much cheaper way of harvesting as a single machine can supposedly harvest thousands of trees per day.

Flotation tanks
The hand picked cherries are then thrown into huge flotation tanks. The cherries with no beans in them, the over-ripe cherries, leaves and sticks all float up to the top and are sometimes netted out by the plantation workers.

The cherries with beans in them all sink to the bottom.

Hand sorting
The cherries that have sunk to the bottom of the tank are then lifted up to a conveyor belt or to a table where they are sorted. Good plantations ensure that almost no green cherries make it past this stage. Roasting up green beans from green cherries tends to make the finished product more bitter.

Separating the Cherry Husk from the Green Beans

The most common way that the green beans are extracted from the cherry is the fermentation or 'wet' method. Without getting too technical, the outer skin of the cherry is first slipped off the cherry by a machine, then the cherry is placed into a concrete or plastic tank, which has natural enzymes and bacteria in it. These enzymes and bacteria separate the husk from the beans. This process can take up to 48 hours.

The beans are then removed from the tank where they have to be washed (about four times) and sun-dried. This involves the beans being placed on concrete or brick terraces or on large trays which sit above ground level, where they are raked over periodically by hand.

Within four days they are then dry and are run through a hulling machine (similar to that shown below) which removes the parchment-like skin and silver skin.

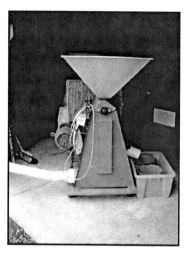

The beans can then be graded firstly by size and then by colour. The latter process is still to this day pretty much done by hand.

Often family groups in these coffee-producing countries gather around large tables and pick the discoloured and defective beans from the good beans. (The good beans are what coffee wholesalers around the world end up with). After the hand sorting is complete, the green coffee beans are placed in their characteristic 60kg (132lbs) hessian bag and sent to the co-op for sale.

Roasting

The specialty roasting machine is rather simple in its operation. It is about three metres high (10ft), is gas driven and is capable of roasting about 20kg (44lbs) to 80kg (176lbs) of coffee at a time.

At the top of the roaster there is an inverted cone called a *hopper* which corrals the green beans. Under the hopper is the central roasting chamber which is essentially a stainless steel tumbler that reaches 210°C (410°F). When the roaster is happy with the temperature in the roasting chamber he/she releases a lever near the hopper that allows the beans to fall into the chamber. The beans then roast for about fourteen minutes, being churned in a motion similar to clothes in a tumble dryer. During the roast the roaster will continually pull out from the roasting chamber a small spoon-like implement (called a trier) which brings with it a sample of the roasting beans. When the roaster is happy with the colour and aroma of the sample beans, he/she pulls another lever further down the machine, which allows all the beans from the roasting chamber to fall into a cooling tray which sits below. The cooling tray has several rotating arms that spread the beans out over small holes through which cool air is forced from below. The beans must cool quickly otherwise they will retain a smoky aroma and will keep 'cooking'. They must go from 210°C (410°F) to sub 40°C (104°F) very quickly.

After about five to ten minutes this process is complete. Another lever down near the cooling tray is then lifted, thus allowing the beans to fall down a small chute and into a bucket, whereupon the roaster prepares the beans for packaging.

Beans lose moisture during the roasting process (about 16%), so that a roaster may put in, say 23 kg (51lbs) but only get 20 kg out (44lbs).

Beans also expand in size so that the resulting brown, roasted bean will be slightly more robust than the green bean it started out as.

The Mega-Roasters

Having toured a state-of-the-art roasting facility in Melbourne recently, we are convinced that even though roasting machines are now incredibly automated and computer-driven, they have in no way taken away the craft that is coffee roasting. Indeed they have been the result of decades of solid development and have culminated in technology that now produces a much more consistent roast. Making coffee roasting and brewing more scientific is not a crime. If it makes the finished product more palatable, we're happy with that.

We have known small roasters to get the odd phone call from cafés saying that they have found nails or even bullets (!) in their beans. There is little chance of this happening with the state-of-the-art roasters spoken of above as the beans are subjected to many sieves before they are finally put into the chamber to roast. Call us old-fashioned but we'd prefer the 1kg (2.2lbs) bags in our cafés to be bullet–free, thank you.

These roasters have sensors within them that can calculate for every batch such details as:
(a) average moisture content of the beans
(b) average bean hardness
(c) average bean density and
(d) average bean size
These four variables combined determine the ideal roasting time.

In the End, It's All in the Blend

Like wine, good coffee is usually a blend of beans from different origins. Most of the coffee we enjoy in our local cafés is blended coffee. The reason roasters blend beans from different places rather than just roasting up green beans from one source is that they end up with something that is much more complex to taste and to smell. For example, Costa Rican coffee might have a very strong taste but it might lack a certain aroma and that is why a Papua New Guinean bean might be added to the blend.

For the above reasons be on guard when coffee houses promote their *coffee of the week* as 'Brazilian' or 'Tanzanian' or some other single origin bean. You may not like the taste from these single origin beans. Our palates have become used to complex blends. However, by all means try them, but view your $3.00 purchase as an experiment rather than a potentially uplifting experience.

Having said this, most *decaf* coffees use Colombian beans as this is one single origin bean that can stand on its own. Colombian beans produce a balance of rich taste, full body and mild acidity. Their large, evenly-sized beans yield a clean, well-rounded, mellow and nicely balanced cup.

If you ever have the privilege of tasting Jamaica Blue Mountain coffee, you will similarly be amazed at how complex-tasting this coffee is. It is however, one of the few single origins that we believe can truly be enjoyed on its own.

Blending Before or After Roasting

To create a coffee company's unique taste, it is not uncommon for 2-8 different types of Arabica and sometimes Robusta beans to be blended together *before* roasting. Beans can be blended *after* roasting but a lot of boutique roasters argue that it is more consistent to blend the green beans before roasting so that the beans all enjoy one consistent roast. We know a large roaster that has certain blends that are created before roasting and certain blends that are created after roasting the individual origins. It really depends on the size, water content, density and hardness of the different beans in the blend. If they are markedly different, the individual origins are usually roasted separately and then blended. To blend before they are roasted would probably result in some beans being 'overcooked' and some being 'undercooked'.

Organic Coffee

This 'new age' coffee is coming to a café near you. Roasters are now roasting beans from countries whose plantations have been certified by relevant government authorities as 'chemical free'. Even the local roasting and packaging must comply with their strict guidelines. Proper organisations even check that the rodent spray used on the perimeter of the roasting plant is chemical-free!

What does 'organic coffee' actually mean? In simple terms it means that the very basic organic agricultural procedures have been adhered to: composting, organic pest control etc.

Technically the land must have been free of synthetic pesticides or fertilisers for the past three years.

Mexico and Peru have long been growing 'organic' coffee but East Timorese organic coffee is now being seen and do you know what? - it isn't a bad brew either. We also feel that in supporting East Timorese coffee we might be helping that economy get back on its feet after years of turmoil. Everyone wins.

Interestingly, the East Timorese coffee is predominantly grown under the canopy of huge trees. Instead of getting direct sunlight, the trees get filtered sun. This is unusual for arabica coffee trees, but the East Timorese do it this way and the coffee is fantastic.

Medium v Full Roasts

The difference between a medium and full roast is about two minutes in the roaster. It sounds like a bad joke, but it's true. You can have the same blend of beans and produce many different shades of the finished roasted bean simply by leaving it to churn around in the roaster for longer. The two that are most commonly sold by wholesalers however, are medium and full roasts.[3]

---

[3] Note that 'full roasts' are sometimes referred to as 'dark roasts'

The medium roast will result in beautiful brown, chocolate-looking beans. The taste will be smooth. The beans will be higher in acidity than in darker roasts.

The full roast will produce comparatively darker, slightly more brittle beans that will contain less moisture than their medium counterparts. An oilier exterior will be seen on the beans. The taste will be stronger than the medium roast, approaching a more 'bittersweet' or tangy flavour. Hopefully the roaster has not allowed the bean to roast until it gets truly bitter, although if you were in France, you would probably appreciate drinking espresso from such charcoal-like beans.

Interestingly full roasts have less caffeine than medium roasts.

We sell full roast coffee to cafés whose clientele is more used to a European flavour. Which one do you prefer?

Bean Freshness
Coffee that has been roasted locally and delivered within 48 hours of it being roasted is going to be as fresh as you can ever get. It is this freshness which is paramount in gourmet coffee. Roasted coffee that has been travelling from overseas in a container for two months is simply not going to cut it in the freshness department.

Roasted beans are good for about 2-3 weeks before they start losing freshness. This is why good roasters will put their beans into bags that have a one-way valve on them. This valve allows carbon dioxide to escape but does not allow oxygen in.

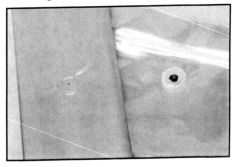

Ultraviolet light and moisture are also enemies of coffee. To maintain optimum freshness, wholesalers should probably be delivering to cafés on a weekly basis.

Cafés should train staff to empty the hopper on top of their grinder every night and put the beans into an airtight container. This way, the beans are not exposed to air overnight. The beans can simply be put back into the hopper the next morning before the café opens.

Ground Coffee Freshness
Forget the old-wives' tales of coffee having to go in the fridge or freezer to maintain freshness.

This thinking amongst gourmet coffee lovers went out with 'roadhouse' froth on cappuccinos.

The reasons you wouldn't put coffee in the fridge or freezer are twofold. First of all, if the container is not completely airtight (and most aren't) the ground coffee will attract moisture which will cause it to go stale more quickly. Secondly, the ground coffee will absorb any other aromas which are in the fridge or freezer. So if you put ground coffee next to a piece of fish it will absorb the aroma of the fish and vice versa. Coffee-tasting fish might be OK but fishy coffee is not our cup of tea. In addition to this drinking coffee from frozen grinds or beans is like hacking into a frozen steak – you just wouldn't do it. The freezer will freeze the oil molecules in coffee and it's this oil that produces the crema. Coffee therefore needs to be at room temperature.

Remember these golden rules. Store coffee:
(1) in an airtight container
(2) away from heat
(3) away from light (in a dark place) and
(4) away from humidity

Getting to Know Your Espresso Machine and Grinder

Like any industry you have to get used to the jargon and the technical terms before you can begin to communicate with anyone else 'in the know.' You won't get far by calling the espresso machine "that big, metal coffee maker-thingy over there." The appropriate terminology being used today can be found in the pages that follow.

[1] Anatomy of the Espresso Machine

Starting from the top and moving down, the following are the main components of the commercial espresso machine:

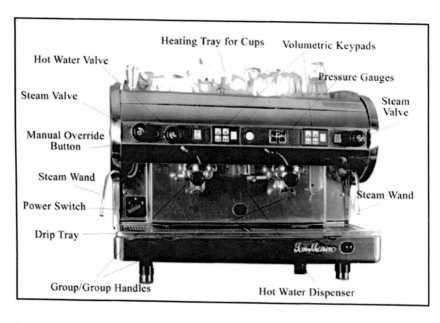

Heating Tray for Cups: where the cups are corralled. Good baristas draw their cups from here when making coffees. Using warm cups enables the coffee to retain its heat better than if cold cups are used.

Steam Valve or Knob: turning this will cause steam to emit from the steam wand. It is the injection of this steam that "stretches" or aerates the milk to create froth.

Hot Water Valve or Knob: turning this will cause boiling water to emit from the hot water dispenser. This hot water is used for long blacks, teas or to clean things.

Manual Override Button: this button when pressed causes hot water to flow from the group until it is turned off again. This button is supposedly there in case the computer board in the machine ever malfunctions and renders the volumetric buttons useless. However, we have never seen this happen. We use the manual override button to wash the group handle before throwing fresh grinds in to make the next cup.

Volumetric Keypad: when pressed, the buttons on this keypad cause a pre-set amount of hot water to flow from the group onto the compacted coffee in the filter basket. This then creates the espresso.

Pressure Gauges: the pressure gauges on most machines measure the pressure of the water tank as well as the pressure that is forced through the espresso. The pressure for brewing should be between 9-10 atmospheres (approximately 132 pounds per square inch).

Group: place where group handle is inserted. It contains shower screen through which hot water is dispensed.

Group Handle: movable handle which contains the filter basket where ground coffee sits.

Hot Water Dispenser: place where boiling water is emitted. This water is used in the making of long blacks, tea or cleaning things.

Steam Wand: long metal tube with nozzle attached to the end which brings out steam from the machine to heat up and froth milk.

Power Switch: you can leave the machine on overnight so that it is ready the next morning, but we prefer to turn it off and open the steam wands to de-pressurise the espresso machine. The machine will take about 10-15 minutes to heat up once turned on.

Drip Tray: collects spilt coffee or water and is often connected to a tube which leads to a wastage bucket under the machine or directly to the sewerage system.

[2] Anatomy of the Grinder

Starting from the top and moving down, the following are the main components of the commercial grinder:

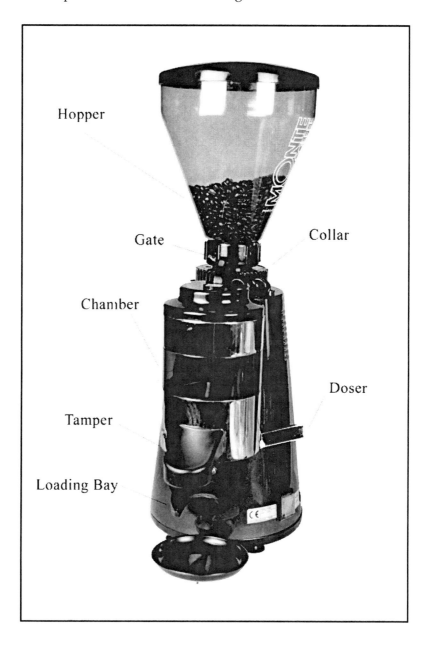

Hopper: where the beans are placed. They continuously fall due to gravity and come into contact with the spinning blades when the grinder is turned on. The hopper holds about 1kg (2.2lbs) of beans. Ensure you keep it clean otherwise the oil builds up with fragments from the beans and you end up looking like a filthy take-away shop that has no idea about cleanliness!

Gate: the thin metal or plastic stopper which slides over the hole at the bottom of the funnel on the hopper and stops beans from falling down due to gravity. It is always a good idea to close the gate when lifting the hopper, otherwise you will be scooping up beans from the floor and counter for a long time. Embarrassing when it happens, all baristas do it at least once in their career.
Collar: the spinning dial that alters the distance between the blades, which in turn adjusts the grind of the coffee. Once you get used to which direction to turn it to adjust the grind you won't need to take the hopper off to look at the picture on it.

Chamber: the cylindrical "holding yard" for the ground coffee. Take a look inside it when it is empty. You can see six or so triangular 'sectors' at the bottom. When full they should each contain 7g (0.25oz) of coffee.

Doser: long metal lever coming out from the bottom right hand side of the grinder. One complete pull of this lever when set correctly will 'dose' or 'throw' out enough ground coffee for one cup of coffee. This should be 7g (0.25oz) of coffee. We know some cafes that try to be extra smart and have two throws for a single shot and three for a double, but sorry folks, it doesn't take a mathematical giant to work out that this just doesn't make sense.

Go and make yourself a cup of coffee then read on. This sounds complex, but stay with us…

If a throw = 7g (0.25oz) (the internationally accepted amount for a standard 8oz coffee) then two throws = 14g (0.5oz) (the internationally accepted amount for two standard 8oz coffees). So if you set the grinder so that it throws out 7g per throw, you wouldn't want to do two throws (14g) for a single shot and three (21g) for a double. Even if you set the grinder so that say, only 5g came out per throw, if you were employing the "two throws for a single shot and three for a double" philosophy you would be getting 10g for a single shot and 15g for a double. We're sorry but if you are making two coffees you would want to double the amount of ground coffee going in to making them, not multiply it by 1.5. (You set the throw to 7g by turning the dosage screw in the centre of the chamber – anti-clockwise to increase the weight or clockwise to reduce the weight. Use a finely calibrated electronic scale when measuring the output of each throw).

If you ever have a spare couple of minutes it is worth taking a look at what happens inside the chamber when you pull the doser. Each pull brings a new triangular sector to the front section of the chamber where there is no 'floor' so that whatever is pushed into it, falls out the bottom (hopefully into the basket in your group handle). That sector will now be empty as it has dropped its load. With each throw thereafter that sector will come closer to being at the point where it will fill up again when it is right underneath the chute where the newly ground coffee falls. Like an assembly line it then travels, now full, around to the front again where eventually it will drop its load.

You will know just by observing this process that obviously if these sectors are not full 7g of ground coffee will not come out with each throw. This will affect the timing and therefore the taste of the espresso. Therefore always operate with the sectors full. If in doubt, look through the window on the chamber to see how much ground coffee is in there. Most machines are automatic anyhow so will always keep the chamber full. (Note: You must be in a very busy café though to need to have your chamber full – remember that good gourmet coffee starts with freshly ground coffee. Ground coffee that has been in the chamber for over half an hour before it comes out is going to be stale coffee!

Tamper: the hunk of plastic that protrudes out from the bottom of the chamber. When you place your group handle under it and apply upwards pressure so that the round part of the tamper compacts the ground coffee in the basket you end up with a nice even compaction. This will aid in the extraction process once the handle is inserted into the group on the machine. Having compacted coffee makes it harder for the water from the group to filter through the ground coffee in the basket. In making it harder it carries with it more flavour on its journey into your cup. Without tamping, the water finds it a breeze to pass through the ground coffee and your espresso ends up coming out very quickly (i.e. much less than 30 seconds) and looks like dirty water rather than rich espresso with a full honeycomb crema on top.

Loading Bay: located at the base of the grinder it is where you place the group handle so that when you pull the doser the ground coffee is dispensed right into the basket.

Using an External Tamper – Let's get Serious

The hunk-of-plastic tamper connected to your commercial grinder is OK and really quite useful in a busy cafe, but it's not perfect and a true barista will not use one. Instead they will use a shiny, aluminium or stainless steel tamper, which entails them applying *downward* pressure onto the coffee in the filter basket.

These tampers aren't cheap at between $20-$40, but they're worth it. We've recently expanded our range of tampers. Our Black Diamond Tampers are top shelf and you won't have to sell your car to pay for them.

(Handy hint: don't put tampers in the dishwasher – they discolour).

For more information on how to use the external tamper, see Chapter 5.

The Daily Grind

All over the country this morning chances are the following conversation took place at the local café…

Café Worker:	"Hey boss! I think there's something wrong with the grind. The coffee is pouring out really, really slowly."
Manager/Owner:	"I told you! Don't touch the grinder! Let the coffee company guy do it next time he's in."

We estimate that probably 90% of 'baristas' do not know how to adjust the grind of the coffee to achieve the optimal espresso. You can have the best beans that money can buy, have the most expensive coffee machine, be a brilliant frother of milk and pour like a true champion, but if your espresso isn't up to scratch, your coffee will be a dud.

We've all had 'weak' or 'watery' coffee. We've all had 'bitter' or 'burnt' coffee. Chances are, the coffee grind was at fault. All it would have taken was a fine-tuning of the coffee grinder by the barista in charge of the coffee making to rectify the situation.

The students at our Barista Basics™ Coffee Academy love seeing latte art and snazzy presentation techniques, but what really blows them away is the '30ml-in-30second' rule. It's simple and it goes like this:

The optimal time that a shot (30ml = 1 fl oz) of espresso should pour out of the spout on the group handle is 30 seconds. If it takes less than this, the grind is too coarse. If more, it is too fine.

At around 30 seconds, the extraction is just long enough for the water passing through the compacted coffee to bring out the good elements, but not too long as to extract the bad, or bitter, elements.

A Daily Ritual
Setting the grinder needs to be a daily ritual. No single setting will be good forever, as the coffee pour will vary according to the humidity that is in the air (and to a lesser extent the temperature and the atmospheric pressure).

Effects of Weather on Extraction Rates
Coffee is hygroscopic, which means it absorbs water. This means that in more humid weather the ground coffee in the filter basket will be more tightly packed. This makes for fewer air holes in the compacted coffee and it will therefore be more difficult for the water to pass through than if the coffee had not absorbed this water from the surrounding humidity. This makes the pour slower so to compensate for this you will need to make the grind coarser.

Rule of thumb:
More humid day = make coffee grind coarser.

Getting technical
The extraction should be approximately 20 seconds for a single or double Ristretto, and should be 26-30 seconds for a single or double Espresso shot. The time is measured from the time the machine pump is activated.

There should be about a four-second delay after you have activated the brew button before the espresso appears. The flow will be smooth with a rich, honeycomb, golden-brown crema.

If the grind is too coarse: the coffee will flow after a couple of seconds and the extraction will be too fast (under 20 seconds). The flow will be noticeably fast and the coffee will be sour, watery and weak and the crema will be pale and dissipate quickly.

If the grind is too fine: the coffee will flow after 5 seconds, the extraction will be very slow (over 30 seconds). The crema will be very dark and the coffee will taste burnt and bitter. Pale bubbly patches and a dark streak in the crema indicate over-extraction. The coffee grinds will also be wet and sludgy.

Rule of thumb:
-    *if the coffee is flowing too quickly, you must make the grind finer*
-    *if the coffee is flowing too slowly, you must make the grind coarser*

How Do I Adjust the Grinder?
Your boss may not want you tampering with the grinder so do it when he/she is at the blender making a frappe or is ducking into the display fridge to pull out some caramel slice for a customer.

What you need to do is go to the collar of the grinder. It is the round 'dial' which sits under the bean hopper. Most grinders come with 'parallel blades' which are two flat, spinning metal wheels that have teeth that spin around, one on top of the other when the grinder is turned on. The teeth face each other and everything caught between them gets ground up and ejected into the ground coffee chamber. Depending on which way you turn the collar, you will be moving the top blade either closer to the bottom one, or further apart.

Now you will probably need to take the hopper off the first time you adjust the grind as you will need to take a good look at the collar *(Handy hint: close the gate on the hopper or beans will fall out as you lift it)*. On the collar, you should see a picture indicating which way to turn it to make the grind coarser and which way to turn it to make the grind finer.

Two examples of such pictures are below and they are fairly typical of most grinders out there:

Think mathematically now. With the above grinder, if we turn the collar clockwise in the negative direction it means that our particle size is getting smaller (i.e. our grind is getting finer). If we turn anti-clockwise in the positive direction, it means that our particle size is getting larger (i.e. our grind is getting coarser).

Logic tells us that with the above grinder, turning the collar in the clockwise direction so that we are approaching the tip of the arrow, our grind would be getting smaller (i.e. finer) and turning it in the anti-clockwise direction so that we are approaching the fat end, our grind would be getting larger (i.e. coarser).

Some grinders have it written in multiple languages which way is coarser and which way is finer. If only all were like this!

Don't worry about the numbers on the collar – they don't mean much and can't really be used as any reference point. It is the picture that is important.

With most grinders, to make the grind finer you need to turn the collar clockwise. To make coarser, you need to turn it anti-clockwise. This is not always the case though, and it does really depend on which country your grinder is from as to which way you need to turn it to make the desired adjustment.

With most grinders, you usually cannot just 'turn' the collar. They are engineered so that baristas and even customers cannot accidentally knock them during the day and change the grind. You will need to depress a button that is connected to the collar with your index finger on one hand, whilst turning the collar with the other. When you have reached the desired setting take your index finger off this button and the collar will naturally 'lock' into place. You shouldn't be able to turn the collar now that the button is no longer depressed.

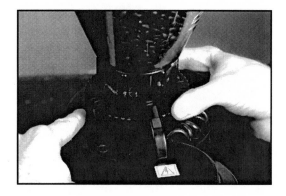

How Often Should I Adjust the Grind?
After tipping out the first couple of espressos in the morning, (the machine is still warming up and there may be some traces of espresso machine cleaner coming out in the espresso from last night's back wash), you should time the pour using a stopwatch. Use the double group handle as it is better for timing purposes than the single.

Once you are in the 26-30 second 'zone' your grind should be OK. But you should keep your eye on it during the day and 'fine tune' if necessary. It will not be unusual to have to change the grind ever so slightly during the day. The weather conditions will no doubt change as the day progresses and the impact that this has on the timing of the pour will be more pronounced the more exposed you are to it (eg. outside operating from a coffee cart).

If your café has two shifts ensure that one of the duties that the second shift barista does is a timing of the pour.

Ever noticed the stopwatches magnetically stuck to the face of espresso machines at some cafés? They're not for show. The barista is periodically timing the pour from the double group handle to maintain the 30 second pour.

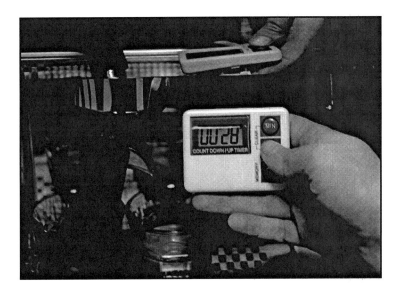

For more insight into this critical part of coffee-making, visit www.baristabrothers.com and listen to our award winning podcast series.

Preparing for the Shot

Step One – Dose out the Required Amount of Ground Coffee from the Chamber

With your group handle in the loading bay pull the doser once if you have a single group handle and twice if you have a double.

Step Two – Even out the Coffee in the Filter Basket

Now that you have dosed out the desired amount of coffee from the grinder the next thing you need to do is try to even out the coffee in the filter basket. Try and make it as flat as you can and definitely leave it so that you cannot see the metal bottom of the filter basket at any point. Remember that you are trying to give the water the best chance of having an *even* extraction through the compacted coffee.

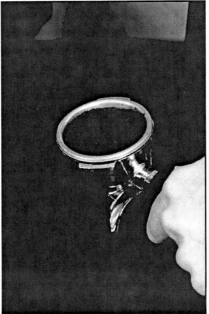

Water takes the path of least resistance so don't make it easy for it to flow out of any one particular spot and underextract the rest of the coffee in the basket – ensure that when the water is dispersed from the shower screen into the group it flows through the filter basket nice and evenly and therefore takes with it the flavour from *all* the coffee, not just a portion of it.

You even out the coffee by quickly moving from side to side the hand that is holding the group handle so that the coffee evens out in the basket. Don't do it too violently so that the ground coffee falls out of the basket. Most people however are too hesitant at this stage and don't tend to shake the group handle enough. Doing a 'fairy shake' will mean that you will fail in this crucial stage of espresso preparation.

You can use your little finger as an alternative to the shake to even out the coffee but we prefer not to have anyone touching the coffee too much with their bare hands if they can help it.

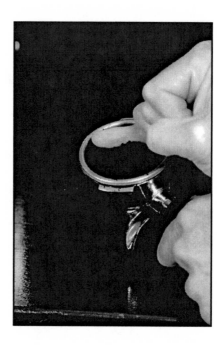

Step Three – Apply Downwards Pressure

Whilst resting the group handle on a bench with one hand, take the tamper with the other hand and apply downwards pressure onto the coffee. The tamper will be slightly smaller in diameter than the filter basket, so you will be able to put the whole bulbous part of the tamper right into the filter basket. Apply approximately 18kg (40lbs) of pressure downwards. *(Handy hint: try to apply 18kg of pressure on your bathroom scales at home to get a "feel" for how much pressure this is).* Try to apply this pressure evenly from right above and twist the tamper as you pull the tamper up and away from the filter basket.

Your coffee is now compact but the tamping process is not finished.

Step Four – Knock Coffee From Sides of Filter Basket into the Middle

This step, in conjunction with Step 5 is where the external tamping method really comes into its own.

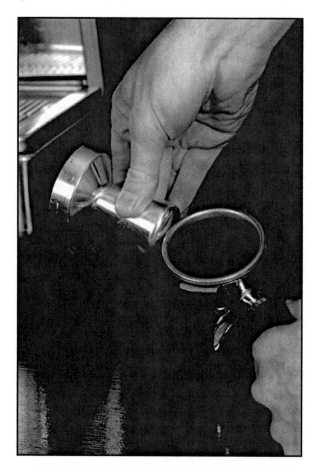

Take the small end of the tamper (the bit that was in the palm of your hand as you tamped last time) and gently tap it on the side of the filter basket (don't use the large end that just compacted the coffee – keep this smooth and dent-free). This light tapping will knock any ground coffee that has been compacted on the top sides of the basket back into the middle.

Step Five – The Light Follow-Up Tamp

Using the large end of the tamper *a la* Step 3 tamp the compacted coffee again, this time using only a very light pressure from above. You are now aiming to compact all of those grinds which have just been bounced back into the middle of the basket from Step 4 above.

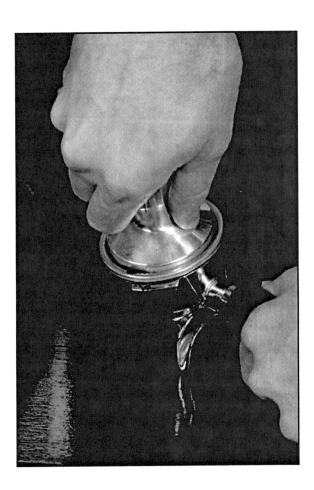

You should now have a smooth layer of coffee with no residue sticking to the sides of the basket.

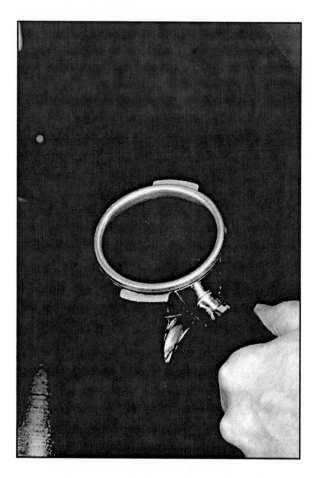

This will give the water the best chance for an even extraction and hence will create a better tasting espresso than using the hunk-of-plastic tamping method.

Oh yes! You will also look more professional using this method.

Step Six – Clean Off Any Grinds on Rim of Filter Basket

With one swipe of the palm of your hand over the rim of the filter basket remove any coffee grinds as these will act like sandpaper when the group handle is inserted into the group and will come into contact with the machine's rubber seal.

Step Seven – Insert the Group Handle into the Group

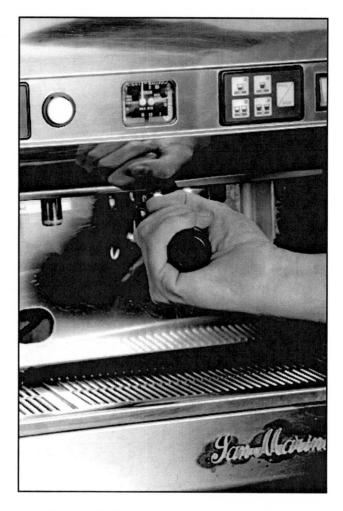

Approach at 45° and lock the group handle into the group. You will feel it naturally locking in. Pull the handle so that it is perpendicular to the machine (or as much as it will turn). It must be inserted with a reasonable amount of force so that it does not leak during the pour but do not force the group handle as this will wear down the seal too much.

A Final Word on Grinders

We have assumed throughout this chapter that you are all working on 'flat burr' or 'parallel blade' grinders. Most grinders have these.

A few new ones however have a different type of blade. These grinders instead of having two blades that work in tandem with each other, have one blade. This type of grinder is called a 'conical burr' or 'conical blade' grinder. The cone-shaped blade grinds against a stationary grinding surface. It has longer cutting edges and can create particles with larger surface areas than the parallel blades can. The blade can therefore rotate at lower speeds than its parallel blade counterpart and hence less friction is created. Because less friction is created, the ground coffee is less affected by heat and therefore in theory, fresher than coffee ground by a parallel blade grinder. These grinders also clog less and are more tolerant of oily coffees.

Conical blade grinders are more expensive however and to be honest are still rarely seen in cafés.

Don't worry though - the same rules for adjusting the grind etc. still apply.

Pouring the Espresso Shot

Chapter 4 explained the importance of the grind of the coffee in achieving a 30ml-in-30second pour.

This chapter explains just how you get 30ml (1 fl oz) in the first place and then goes on to describe what you should be seeing as the espresso pours out into the coffee cup.

Achieving A Perfect 30ml (1 fl oz) Shot - Volumetric Machines
If you have a volumetric machine (i.e. one that has a computer board that regulates the flow of water so that it pours out the same volume every time), you can program it to dispense 30ml (1 fl oz) for a single pour and 60ml (2 fl oz) for a double.

Getting to Know Your Keypad
The machine will almost always have four pictures of coffee cups on the keypad.

[1] One short black – (top left button in picture above) press to get one espresso shot (30ml = 1 fl oz). Ensure you have a single filter basket in a single group handle.
[2] Two short blacks – (bottom left button in picture above) press to get two espresso shots (30ml+30ml = 60ml = 2 fl oz).
Ensure you have a double filter basket in a double group handle.

[3] One long black – (top right button in picture on previous page) don't program this for a long black. This is an incorrect way of producing a long black. See Chapter 8 on Coffee Drinks and Other Orders.

We prefer to program this button for a single ristretto shot (20ml = 0.7 fl oz). This way we can press this button when someone wants a ristretto, or more frequently when someone wants a *weak* coffee. We simply dispense the 20ml shot and use this as the espresso base for the drink. So, for example, if someone wants a weak cappuccino we would pour a ristretto shot (which, by the way, if the grind is correct, should come out in 20 seconds), and add milk and froth and chocolate sprinkles as usual. The resulting drink has less volume of espresso in it and is therefore 'weaker.'

(You could achieve the weak drink by using a standard shot and taking the cup away before the machine has finished pouring the 30ml out but this is both messy and unscientific).

Of course when pouring a single ristretto use the single filter basket and the single group handle.

[4] Two long blacks – (bottom right button in picture on previous page) don't program this for two short blacks. This is an incorrect way of producing two long blacks. See Chapter 8 on Coffee Drinks and Other Orders.

We prefer to program this button for two ristretto shots (20ml +20ml = 40ml).

Of course when pouring a double ristretto use the double filter basket and the double group handle.

Programming the Machine
It's not rocket science but once it's done to your specifications, you never have to change it. The machine has a computer chip in it which ensures that the same volume of water and hence espresso is dispensed every time.

Example: Programming the machine for a short black

[1] Load up a single group handle with a single filter basket as you would normally (i.e. with 7g = 0.25oz of coffee).

[2] Insert it into the group.

[3] Place a 50ml (1.75 fl oz) measuring cylinder under the spout (a plastic medicine one bought for $2 at the pharmacy is fine).

[4] Press the 'fifth' button on the keypad (other than the four coffee cup pictures spoken of above). This puts you in program mode. This fifth button may be a star symbol or something similar or may indeed have the word 'Prog/Stop' or 'Program' written on it. When you press it a green light will usually appear above the four coffee cup pictures.

[5] As soon as you press the fifth button in step [4] above, press the button containing the coffee cup you want to program. In this case you want to program the short black button so press it. Espresso will start to pour out. When the level of the espresso reaches 30ml, press the fifth button again, and this will stop the pouring.

An alternative to step [5] is to place fine digital scales underneath the single group handle that has already been loaded into the espresso machine. Put a demitasse cup on the scales and zero it. As soon as you have pressed the fifth button in step [4] press the button containing the coffee cup you want to program. In this case you want to program the short black button, so press it. The espresso is now pouring from the spout into the cup sitting on the scales. Wait until the scales reach 30g = 1oz (30ml weighs 30g you see!) Press the fifth button again and this will stop the pouring. If you have exactly 30g on the scales you will have 30ml of espresso. This method of programming is considered by some to be superior to the measuring cup method as it avoids complications with measuring volume where crema is involved (it is difficult to judge 30ml during a pour into a small measuring cup because the crema is still settling).

Your short black button will now be programmed for all time. This means that every time you hit this button, you will get out 30ml of espresso. Whether it comes out in 30 seconds is then up to your grind.

Repeat the above steps for all the coffee cup buttons you want to program. You will notice that each time you press the fifth button to program a new button, less green lights appear above the coffee cup buttons. The ones already programmed will not light up.

(Handy hint: Remember to use a double group handle for double coffee buttons you are programming and put the measuring cylinder under one of the spouts and still measure 30ml).

Machine Anomalies
Some machines like the San Marino have a switch under the heating tray for cups at the top of the machine. Just unscrew the front screws and lift the grill to reveal the inner workings of the machine. On the right hand side of the top of the machine, just under where the grill sat you will see a switch that says 'on' on one side of the switch movement. If your switch is flicked to 'on' you are in program mode and can then program the machine as usual. It is a safety mechanism so that your first-day-on-the-job-casual doesn't by some miracle press the keypad in the correct sequence and throw out your programmed dosages. The machine must be in program mode to set the keypad.

Once everything is set, flick this switch to the off position and screw on the grill again. You shouldn't have to touch this switch ever again as your machine is now programmed. Importantly, nobody can tamper with your settings unless this switch is turned back to the 'on' position.

Achieving a Perfect 30ml (1 fl oz) Shot - Manual Machines
If you are operating one of these slightly older types of espresso machines and do not have the luxury of having a perfect shot poured out every time at the hit of a button, you have to use the manual override button to dispense espresso. Every time the espresso pours, you must visually assess the volume and switch the button to the off position when you think 30 ml (1 fl oz) has poured.

This method is obviously not scientific and unless you are a pro the amount will vary every time and therefore your espresso may be too concentrated or not strong enough but rarely perfect.

We recommend that people using these manual machines should buy a measuring cylinder from a local pharmacy for $2 and measure 30ml of espresso, then pour it into the cups they are using to get a 'feel' for what 30ml looks like in their cup. This should help in the judging of the 30ml pour thereafter.

What to Expect as the Espresso Pours Into the Coffee Cup

Let's assume you have the grind worked out (see Chapter 4) and now you know how to get a consistent 30ml shot (see above). Let's look in closer detail at what you should be seeing as the espresso pours out from the spout.

- Zero to four seconds – you should be seeing nothing at all. The water will be infusing through the compacted ground coffee on its journey through to the spout and then into the cup. If you see espresso a second or so after you press the button, your grind is too coarse (or you don't have enough coffee in the filter basket).

- Five to six seconds – rich drops of espresso pouring out faster and faster.

- Six to twenty eight seconds - 'spaghetti in the wind' or an 'inverted rats tail' are two ways to describe the consistency of the espresso as it pours out during this phase. Some people prefer to liken the correct flow of the espresso to 'honey dripping from a spoon.' Basically, you should now be seeing a steady stream of crema-rich espresso pouring out that should not be dripping any more. The stream should be relatively consistent.

- Twenty eight to thirty seconds - rich drops of espresso pouring out slower and slower until no more pours out.

A Quick Note on Water Temperature

The temperature of the water coming through the group and filtering through your compacted ground coffee should be between 92°- 96°C (198°-205°F).

The Finished Product

The espresso should contain a thick layer of honeycomb-coloured 'foam' on top. This is called the crema. (The crema consists of the oils from the coffee and the caffeine. It's also from where a lot of the aroma from the espresso emanates). Underneath will be the rich black liquid part of the espresso. The crema sits on top because oil is lighter than water.

The crema is a good attribute of coffee. If you don't see it, something is wrong. Alternatively if it is there but too dark, patchy or bubby (or all three) something is similarly wrong (in both instances, your problem is probably the grind – see Chapter 4).

The crema should sit on top of the black liquid part of the espresso for a couple of minutes before dissipating.

Preparing for the Next Espresso

You will need to remove the spent coffee from the filter basket before you load in new ground coffee from the grinder. To do this, you need to knock out the pellet in the filter basket. Most cafes have a 'knock box' or 'spent coffee tube' which is essentially a PVC pipe with a cross bar. (If unsure, look for the most dirty object in the café - dripping with coffee and old grinds - and you have probably found it). Knock the group handle head containing the filter basket against the cross bar on the knock box a few times (metal on plastic won't ruin your filter basket) and remove as much spent coffee as you can.

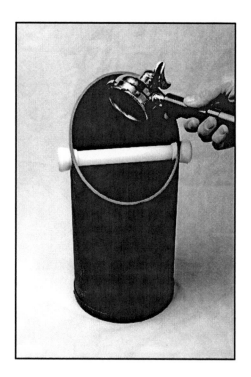

Lift the group handle back to the espresso machine. You will notice that there are some wet coffee grounds still in the basket (i.e. it won't be fully clean). You need to get rid of these grounds as you will not want to dose in fresh grounds and mix them with these bitter, wet ones. To finish cleaning the filter basket, flick the manual override button to the 'on' position and rinse the group handle head top and bottom for a few seconds.

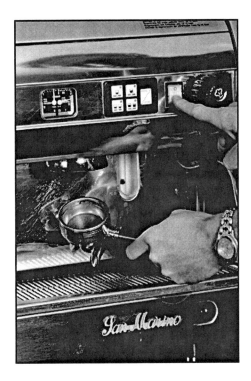

Turn the manual override button to the 'off' position and let the group handle drain over the drip tray for a couple of seconds. Your group handle will now be clean and ready to refill with freshly ground coffee for the next cup.

Don't be lazy and miss this step. We've seen 80kg (176lbs) per week cafés that make this a ritual. This is part of the reason that they are 80kg per week cafés! (By the way, for café novices, 80kg per week is pretty good!)

During the Day
When you are not using the espresso machine do not leave your group handles face down on the drip tray. A lot of restaurants do this. It is not a good idea because they will lose heat and completely cool down. When you reinsert them into the machine and pour espresso through them the espresso loses heat as the group handles absorb it. The result: luke-warm espressos.

Keep the group handles inserted in the machine as shown above. Arguably it is better to have the wet coffee grinds from the last pour still in the baskets, as this will help to keep the handles warm. Some baristas like to knock out the spent coffee, clean the baskets and re-insert them so that they are ready to load up when the next customer comes along. This is fine also.

A Quick Note on Cup Selection
For short black (espresso) or short macchiato use a demitasse cup. Hold the cup close to the spout during the pour if possible, to avoid the splashing marks that occur if you allow the espresso to pour from the spout into a cup sitting down on the drip tray.

For long black, vienna, long macchiato, cappuccino, flat white, steamer, hot chocolate or caffe mocha use a ceramic cup.

For a caffe latte use a glass. (Some baristas use a glass for hot chocolate and caffe mocha and this is perfectly acceptable).

Avoid pouring everything into a shot glass first then transferring to your coffee vessel as the rich crema tends to stick to the shot glass and not get transferred to the customer's cup. Remember the crema is the most tasty part of the espresso.

Always draw your cups from the top of the cappuccino machine as they will be warmer here.

(Handy hint: don't put wet cups or glasses onto the heating tray as water may drip down into the electrical components of the machine. Water and electricity don't mix!)

The Art of Frothing Milk

Understanding and mastering the technique of 'frothing' (these days more aptly called 'texturing') milk is absolutely vital to the making of a great milk-based drink. There is both technique and art involved. The technique you can learn, but the art side will only come with practice and patience.

What we want to achieve is silky, smooth, textured milk - not what we call 'roadhouse' froth. Roadhouse froth has huge, tasteless bubbles that need to be spooned into the cup. Cappuccinos made from roadhouse froth collapse within minutes, leaving the customer with half the cup they used to have. (Of course this style of froth is not confined to roadhouses but is still found in thousands of cafés around the country!)

Cold Milk
You need to start with very cold milk as warm milk will not froth. We have seen some baristas throw ice into their milk jugs before they froth to bring the temperature right down to below fridge temperature. These baristas say that this milk makes excellent froth.

Steam alters the protein in the milk. It is the proteins that fill with hot air and expand to create the froth. Skim milk is easier to froth than full cream milk as it has more proteins. Soy milk is the hardest type of milk to froth.

By following our tips below you will be able to froth all of these with ease.

The Jug
Select a stainless steel jug in a size that is appropriate for the number and type of coffees you need to pour. Generally you will need a 600ml (21 fl oz) jug for two cappuccinos, a 1 litre (35 fl oz) jug for three cappuccinos and so on. (When you start you

may find you need a slightly larger jug than we recommend above as you begin to perfect your frothing technique).

We used to own a café near a university. When the holidays rolled around the café was very quiet. Sometimes our customers were fifteen minutes apart. In these quiet times we would use a small, 600ml (21 fl oz) jug. Imagine if we did what the 'roadhouses' do and used a huge jug and just kept frothing the same milk all day long. Soon we would have had no customers!

Fill the jug up to the halfway mark (this is usually just below where the spout starts to protrude out from the jug). Do not fill beyond this point because when the froth is created it will flow over the top of the jug. (If you do overfill just stop frothing and pour some out into a spare jug and then keep going). Similarly do not fill the jug below this point as your milk will not froth well and will end up having too many large bubbles.

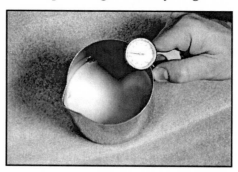

Swirling

Before positioning the milk jug bleed the steam wand to clear the nozzle of water. Do this by turning on the steam valve slightly and purging out the water which normally precedes the steam. The water is from a build up of condensation and will be more prevalent if the wand has not been used for a while.

Now hold the milk jug so that the steam wand is about 1.25cm (0.5 in) into the milk.

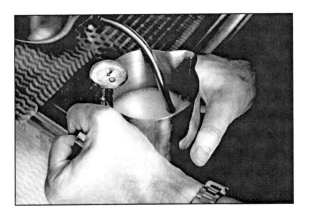

Now fully open up the steam valve. (A partially open steam valve could result in milk being sucked back into the water tank). Generally a steam valve only has to be turned 180-360 degrees to fully open it up. It is best to start with the steam valve fully open as you can always decrease the steam flow if you need to.

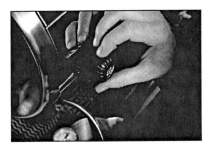

The milk needs to be 'swirling' or rotating in a circular motion in the jug, similar to that of water spinning down the drain in the bathtub. You will need to position the steam wand in the jug so that you achieve this. We find that if you position the wand in a vertical position close to the side of the jug you get the best swirling. We tend to also hold the jug so that the bottom is flat rather than on an angle.

Stretching

Once you get the 'swirling' the bottom of the steam wand nozzle (where the little holes are from which steam emits) should be moved as close to the surface of the milk as possible to allow 'stretching' of the milk. You achieve this by lowering your jug carefully downwards. The milk will now start to take in air and expand rapidly to dense froth. This is usually accompanied by an audible hissing sound.

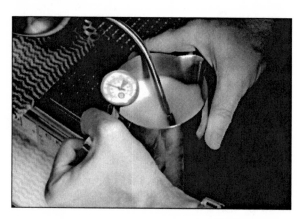

Towards the middle of the frothing process allow the milk to cover the steam wand nozzle completely so that less hissing sound is heard. This will help create a rich texture in the milk and will ensure it does not froth too much. The milk should still be 'swirling' in the jug.

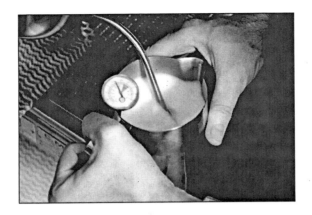

You should aim to complete this frothing operation in about 15 seconds. Always use a thermometer. Aim to have the steam wand fully turned to the off position by the time the thermometer has reached 60°C (140°F). There is a lag on the thermometer which means that by the time you put the jug down to clean the steam wand it will have reached 65°C (150°F).

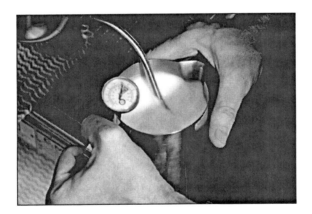

Milk Temperature
If the milk is close to 60°C (140°F), the milk will be the overpowering flavour of the drink. We believe that 65°C (150°F) to 70°C (158°F) is the best temperature for the milk. At this temperature the milk is still flavoursome but the true flavours of the espresso are allowed to shine through. Over 70°C (158°F) the milk becomes thinner and the aroma from the espresso declines. Over 80°C (176°F) the milk scalds and the drink becomes bitter in taste. We have a customer who wants his coffee "hot, hot,

hot". We normally scald his cup with hot water and then put the coffee in at 65°C (150°F). He still gets a great cup of coffee and he feels it is hot as his cup is so hot. Customers who ask for especially hot drinks have probably been disappointed in their coffee temperature at other establishments and now ask for their coffee to be extra hot everywhere they go. You will find that 65°C (150°F) is acceptable to these customers.

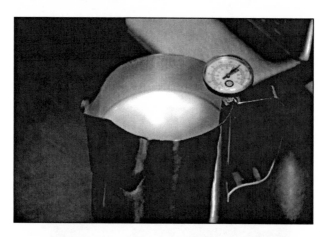

Banging

We usually 'bang' the jug on the counter to dissipate any bubbles. If you have a totally smooth, silky froth you will not need to do this but you will if you have any visible bubbles on top of the milk after you have finished frothing. You can also rotate the milk in the jug by moving the wrist holding the jug in a circular motion. This brings up any bubbles under the surface and keeps the milk creamy. Bang the jug on the counter again to remove the air bubbles that are now on the top.

The milk is now ready to pour.

Pouring

Always pour first the coffee that needs the most amount of froth. So if the order is for a cappuccino and a latte you would pour the cappuccino first. We find it best to pour into the centre of the cup or glass. If you pour as soon as you finish frothing you will not need to 'spoon out the froth.' We use a small spatula to guide the froth out as we pour. How much froth we guide out will depend on what drink we are making. With practice you will get to the stage that you do not even need to use a spatula. You will just 'free pour' and end up with a great finished product. We prefer to use the spatula, however, for a more presentable finish to our coffees.

Left-Over Milk

We are constantly asked if you can re-use left-over milk. Once again folks, jug selection is vitally important. Because we manage the milk frothed by using different-sized jugs, our left-over milk is minimal. The small amount that is left we do re-use as a matter of practicality. In the tight margin hospitality trade you can't afford to throw out milk. Cooling this milk in the refrigerator is best to get the temperature down and the addition of more fresh milk will help to compensate for the loss of protein during the previous frothing.

Clean the Steam Wand After Each Use

Always wipe clean the steam wand after frothing to prevent the build up of milk in the nozzles. Turn the steam valve on again temporarily to purge the milk that is left in the wand so that the next time it is used stale milk does not come out. Collect this spent milk with a blue wipe cloth.

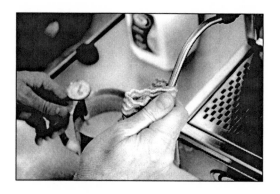

Blue & Green Wipe Cloths

We use two, different coloured wipe cloths in our café. This is for hygiene reasons. The blue coloured wipe cloths are only used on the steam wands. The green coloured wipe cloths are used on all other surfaces (except the floor, where paper wipes are always used). This colour differentiation ensures that our team members do not make the mistake of using a bench cloth on the part of the machine that touches the customers' milk.

Thermometer vs Hand

The traditional method of monitoring the temperature of milk is to put the palm of the hand not holding the handle of the jug on the side of the jug and when the jug is too hot to touch, turn off the steam valve and remove the jug. The problem with this method is that not only is it inaccurate but we find that everyone has a different pain threshold when it comes to holding the hot jug. For example we explained this method to our sister (who delivers babies and has delicate soft hands) and when she practised frothing milk she consistently stopped the frothing at 50°C (122°F). We find in our cafés and our Barista Basics™ classes that a fair percentage of baristas do not even drink coffee so they never taste what they are serving! They might think the milk is hot, but it's not.

The thermometer solves this problem. Everyone in our café uses the thermometers, including the most experienced baristas. And you know what? We never have coffees returned because they are too cold. Consistency is the key to successful coffee-making and a thermometer will take you one step closer to achieving this.

There are Good Days…and Bad Days

Sometimes during the year (generally late summer and autumn) you will find milk hard to froth. It is the increased action of lipase, an enzyme that is found in raw milk that is the cause of this. Lipase acts on the fat found in milk and is known as lipolysis.

The causes of lipolysis

The major cause of lipolysis is the lactation and nutrition of the individual cow. If there is little green feed available we would expect lipolysis to occur due to the cow's poor nutritional standard.

What Can You Do?

Lipolysis is a worldwide problem and one that is difficult to solve particularly under drought conditions. If milk is frothing poorly the first action should be to try using milk of a different batch (eg. different use-by date or pack size) as it is quite likely that the replacement milk will be from a different area. (We use Riverina Milk in our training rooms and it never misses a beat. Test different brands because quality and consistency does differ due to the different processing methods of the various factories producing the different brands).

Sometimes at this time of the year it is good to try using modified milks such as Farmers Best, Lite White, Shape or Balance which by virtue of their slightly higher protein and lower fat content would normally froth better than whole/full cream milk.

(Handy hint: your first port of call should be to clean the steam wand itself as blocked steam holes will reduce its frothing ability. Also investigate whether the correct steam wand has been installed on your machine).

Coffee Drinks and Other Orders

People are always inventing new drinks but we think we have covered all the popular coffees below. We think it is a good idea to have this list posted somewhere in the café so that new staff members can refer to it should they need to. If you are just starting in a café or restaurant take this list with you. It is easy to get flustered when you start working with coffee and this list is bound to save you at some stage. It saved us in our first few weeks behind an espresso machine!

Coffee-Based Drinks

Espresso/Short black
An espresso and a short black are the same thing. It is just a shot of espresso (30ml = 1 fl oz) served in a demitasse cup or glass.

Doppio Espresso
This is two shots of espresso (60ml = 2 fl oz) served in a large espresso glass or cup.

Ristretto
Two thirds of a shot of espresso served in a small cup. The customer who wants this knows that the first 20ml (0.7 fl oz) is the most pure part of an espresso shot. We set our machines so that we can pour this using the volumetric keypad (see Chapter 6 on Pouring the Espresso Shot). It is not that we get asked for a

great deal of ristrettos but we sure get asked for lots of weak coffees and for these we just use the 20ml ristretto shot. Easy!

Short Macchiato
There is a great deal of debate as to how to present a short macchiato. We go for the traditional Italian method. That is, a shot of espresso served in a small cup or glass with a dash of milk and two teaspoons of froth. Use the smoothest, creamiest froth you can get. Put the froth in the centre of the cup using a spoon. It will slowly move out to the side of the cup leaving a nice ring of crema with white froth in the centre.

Cappuccino
We use a standard 240ml (8 fl oz) porcelain cup. Add a single espresso shot and then pour creamy, textured milk on top, extending over the rim to create a 'dome'. Creamy froth should extend down about 10mm (0.4in) below the rim of the cup. (N.B. Top up carefully with milk from the jug if the cappuccino looks flat. This may need to be done if the cappuccino was poured first and fast.) We then sprinkle chocolate drinking powder on the cappuccino. We like to create a design - a checkerboard always looks good.

It may seem cheesy but you can get some great stencil designs at catering shops to create pictures on your cappuccinos (bakers use them too). Our clients love a bit of a change - a heart on Valentines Day - a clover on St Patrick's Day - why not? Have fun - be fun!

Caffe Latte

Caffe lattes are generally served in glasses. At our Barista Basics™ Coffee Academy, we use a 210ml (7 fl oz) French manufactured glass on some occasions we use a 240ml (8 fl oz) Asian manufactured glass. The 210ml (7 fl oz) French glass looks and feels up-market but some people may feel they are not getting the full bang for their buck with this one. It will depend on what you charge and what your location is as to what you use.

We pour a standard espresso shot into a glass. While the shot is pouring texture the milk. Pour as soon as the milk is finished texturing. Pour straight down the centre of the glass and ensure the pour is a constant stream of milk. Start about 10cm (4in) above the glass and steadily move the jug downwards towards the rim of the glass during the pour. We aim for about 1cm (0.4 in) of froth. The froth should meet the top of the glass. We always do some sort of art on our lattes and later we dedicate a whole section to this (see Chapter 12 on Coffee Art).

(Handy hint: for travellers to Italy or France, if you ask for a 'latte' they will just give you hot milk. You must put the word 'caffe' in front of it, to indicate that you want coffee with your milk!)

Flat White (an Australian invention)

How many times do we have to hear the following: "I do not want any froth on my flat white!" We know that 2mm (0.08 in) of froth makes little difference to the taste but it makes all the difference in the world to the presentation of the coffee.

We use the standard 240ml (8 fl oz) porcelain cup. Start with a standard shot of espresso and with your jug down low (it can even rest on the rim of the cup) pour frothed milk down the centre of the cup. Pour slowly so that only a little froth enters the coffee during the pour. A flat white wants a little bit of creamy froth to give the coffee some 'body' but not as much as a caffe latte and definitely not as much as a cappuccino.

Use your thermometer to create a design on the surface of the cup - we usually do a simple swirl starting at the outside of the cup and work our way into the centre. You can then create a simple heart by then running your thermometer from one side of the cup surface to the other.

We advocate the same amount of coffee going into a cappuccino, caffe latte and flat white (one espresso shot or 30ml = 1 fl oz). The milk should also be the same temperature (65°C = 150°F) in each. Essentially the only difference between all three drinks is the amount of froth and whether chocolate powder is sprinkled on top or not.

Caffe Mocha

We love mochas. A mocha is a combination of espresso coffee and chocolate. Start by dissolving one tablespoon of chocolate drinking powder with a shot of espresso. You can serve this in a porcelain cup or a glass. If you are serving in the cup then pour your milk like a cappuccino and if serving in a glass pour as you would a caffe latte. Top with a sprinkling of chocolate drinking powder.

White Caffe Mocha

This is the same as a caffe mocha but we use white chocolate drinking powder. We also mix the white chocolate and the normal chocolate to get our own special mocha and hot chocolate drinks.

Long Black (Americano)

It seems that the most common way of making a long black is to load up the group handle and then run water through it to extract the coffee until it fills the cup. This is WRONG! What you get is an over extracted, bitter coffee.

The best way to make a long black is to start with a regular porcelain cup. Half fill it with hot water or until you are about 3cm (1.2 in) from the top. Then pour in two espresso shots over the water. By putting the espresso shots in last you have a nice crema on top of the long black. We put two shots in our standard 240ml cups. This works for us but it may be too strong for your customers. If this is the case, try two 20ml (2 x 0.7 fl oz) shots or even just one 30ml (1 fl oz) shot. By combining the pure water with the pure espresso shots you create a smooth coffee with no bitter aftertaste. Taste the difference!

Long Macchiato (another Australian creation)

This is like a short macchiato except that the basis for the drink is a long black not an espresso. Take a long black and gently pour in a little hot milk whilst restraining the froth. Then put the jug down and with a large spoon get the smoothest, creamiest froth you can get from the jug and place it into the centre of the cup. You put the froth in the centre of the cup so that it slowly moves out to the side of the cup leaving a nice ring of crema around the edges with white froth in the centre. You may need two tablespoons of this creamy froth to get the right amount of it covering the majority of the surface. See the picture overleaf.

Vienna

A Vienna is a long black served with whipped cream, with chocolate drinking powder sprinkled on top. When you make this drink do not fill the cup with as much hot water as you would normally as the cream melts quickly and ends up pouring over the edge of the cup (and ultimately all over the customers!). You probably won't make too many of these in your barista career as the Vienna really went out with Miami Vice, The Village People and shoulder pads.

Mocha Vienna & White Mocha Vienna

This is the same as a standard Vienna but you mix in one tablespoon of chocolate drinking powder or white chocolate drinking powder with the hot water.

Non Coffee-Based Drinks

Hot Chocolate

Dissolve one tablespoon of chocolate drinking powder with a small amount of hot water or milk. Next pour frothed milk on top and sprinkle with chocolate drinking powder. You can serve this in a porcelain cup or a glass. If you are serving in a cup then pour your milk like a cappuccino and if serving in a glass, pour as you would a caffe latte. If using a glass you can decorate the inside of the glass with fudge. This adds greatly to the presentation of the drink.

Steamer

This is a good one for your menu. It is a shot of flavoured syrup, hot milk and froth (pour as you would a cappuccino) with a sprinkling of chocolate drinking powder. We used to sell lots of these in our cafés, particularly in winter. They are great for people that come into your café and do not want a coffee, yet want a nice hot drink. Someone once described the steamer in one of our barista classes as a 'hot milkshake' – not a bad description!

Babycino

This is simply a demitasse cup filled with froth. Chocolate sprinkles on top are a must. Make sure the froth is fully separated from the milk before you spoon out the froth. You must not scald the toddler's mouth! The best method to use when making a babycino is to froth a small jug of milk and let it sit for a few minutes while you make other drinks. By then, the froth will have separated and you will easily be able to spoon out the froth into the cup.

Marshmallows

Our only tip on marshmallows is to place them on the side of the plate when you serve the drink. If you put them in the drink, they melt and you will get customers coming back asking, "Where are the marshmallows?" This is especially true with babycinos.

A Word on Syrups

Flavoured syrups are now a very popular additive to coffee-based drinks. Having syrups on your menu will expand the menu and add some fun as well. Personally, we both tend to like a caramel latte or a crème brulée latte in the afternoons. The most common syrups we would recommend having on your menu are: Caramel, Chocolate, Hazelnut, Irish Crème and French Vanilla. There are many others. We usually have at least one more flavour on offer. For a standard 240ml cup (8 fl oz) use a 15ml (0.5 fl oz) shot of syrup. Always put the syrup in the cup first, then the espresso shot and then the milk or water. If you do this, the syrup will mix in with the drink and not need any additional stirring.

Pretentious Coffee Styles

Need to impress someone at the espresso bar when placing your order? Try one of these….

Affogato
Scoop of ice cream with one or two hot espresso shots poured over the top and served in a cup.

Piccolo Latte
Small espresso glass filled with a shot of espresso, milk and 5mm (0.2in) of froth. The glass should be slightly bigger than a demitasse cup and filled so that the top of the froth is level with the top of the glass.

Roberto, a barista friend of ours, swears by the warming effect of the alcohol combined with the aromas of coffee after a good meal in his restaurant. The basics of using alcohol with coffee are the same as using syrups with coffee.

There are too many combinations of alcohol and coffee to list but some popular ones we would recommend are as follows:

Irish Coffee
We often order this one. Combine two teaspoons of sugar with a long black and a shot of Irish Whiskey. Top with whipped cream. Serve in a tall latte glass with a handle.

Bailey's Irish Cream Coffee
Use a large wine glass. Pour in 1.5 shots of Bailey's Original Irish Cream, two shots of espresso and add hot water and whipped cream. Top with ground cinnamon.

Café Royale
Scald a large wine glass with hot water to warm. Pour two shots of espresso and hot water into the glass. Add 0.5 teaspoons of sugar. Stir to dissolve. Put a sugar cube and 1.5 shots of brandy in a warm bowl. Ignite the brandy and sugar and pour the contents into the wineglass. Stir once the sugar has dissolved.

Amaretto Coffee
Scald one large brandy glass with hot water to warm. Pour two espresso shots and hot water over 1.5 shots of Amaretto liqueur. Stir and top with whipped cream.

Frangelico Coffee
Scald one wine glass with hot water to warm. Pour two espresso shots and hot water over 1.5 shots of Frangelico liqueur. Stir and top with whipped cream.

The Customer is Always Right?
Well, we let them think they are. Coffee is still developing in many parts of the world and it seems everyone is an expert - your hairdresser, your newsagent, and even your best friend! To our mind if someone wants a flat white with absolutely no froth then that is what we give them. Hold the nicely presented art on top!

Clean your Machine!

The Espresso Machine

We've lost count of the number of cafés that we visit that do not clean their espresso machines properly. In fact there are many out there that do not clean them at all. We can tell just by looking at a machine if this is the case. The real test is always the taste. You just can't get great coffee from a poorly cleaned machine. Sometimes after a clean, our hands will go black from the rancid oils that come from the shower screens and filter baskets.

Rancid flavours will come though in your coffee if the espresso machine is not kept clean. It is important to realise that all surfaces that the coffee touches in the espresso making process need to be cleaned thoroughly.

Filter Baskets

The filter baskets need to be popped out of the group handles and cleaned at least once a day. We use a small scouring pad to do this. A quick scrub with the pad and a rinse is all that is needed. In a busy café this should be done two or three times a day. We soak our baskets overnight in espresso cleaner to keep them like new.

Group Handles (Porta-Filters)

Once the filter baskets have been popped out use the scouring pad to clean the group handles under running water. Then put them into the container with the filter baskets. Do not let the black plastic handles soak as they will crack and eventually fall off (just soak the metallic head).

Back Washing & Shower Screen Cleaning

Your espresso machine should be back washed daily. Regular maintenance will mean less work that technicians have to perform, and it will prolong the life of group parts, including the 3-way solenoid valve.

We do the following every day:

Take the blind filter, attach to group handle and place half a teaspoon of machine cleaner in the blind filter. A blind filter should have been supplied with your machine. It is basically a basket with no holes in it. (If you do not have one just call your coffee supplier and ask them to get one for you). Load the group handle into the group.

Using the manual switch, turn the group on for three-five seconds at a time. (Note: after switching off, watch for the exhaust of froth at the rear of group. This must happen at the end of each operation. The first exhaust will normally be clear water, the second should be white froth, the third should be brown froth). Continue at five-second intervals until the exhaust returns to clear water (approximately 10 times). You may even want to backwash a couple of times after this even though the exhaust looks clear just to ensure all of the machine cleaner has run completely through the system.

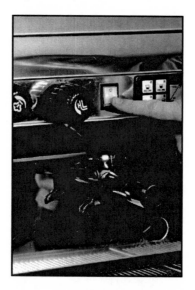

Next, take a small screwdriver and remove the shower screen. Clean it thoroughly with the green scourer. Soak this and the brass underpart in the same container as the filter baskets and group handles. This container should be approximately half-filled with hot water and two teaspoons of machine cleaner should be added. The items in the container should be left to soak for at least 30 minutes (or preferably left overnight).

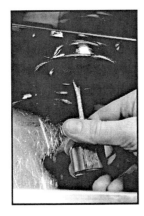

(Handy hint: put the screw from the shower screen in a little demitasse cup on top of the coffee machine along with the screwdriver so that it can be found easily when re-inserting the shower screen.)

Turn the manual switch on each group for 3-5 seconds to expel any white froth left after the shower screens have been removed.

Drip Tray

You will need to remove the drip tray and clean it under warm water. Make sure it is dry before you place it back in the machine. Before you put it back, clean the copper part where the drip tray usually lies with a wipe cloth as there is often a build up of milk and water here.

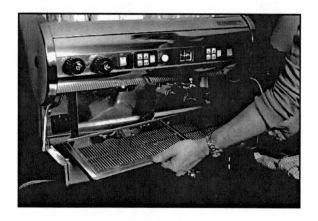

Steam Wands

Wipe the steam wands and make sure that the holes at the bottom of the wands are open and clean. If they are blocked just use the end of a paper clip to clear them. If the tips of the wands actually wind off, do this each day to make sure the wand is fully clean.

Final Buff

The last thing we do each day is buff up our espresso machine using paper towels and stainless steel cleaner or window cleaner (one of our students has even suggested that the best cleaning solution is a mixture of one third methylated spirits and two thirds vinegar). After this we give the machine a final buff up with a polishing cloth. The cloth can be easily purchased at most supermarkets. Our aim is to make the machine shine and look as though it is brand new. One indicator to our customers that we are passionate about our coffee is the fact that all our equipment looks brand new.

Turn off the Machine

Some cafés leave the machine on all night so it is ready to go in the morning as soon as they arrive. This is fine. With small espresso machines that take a great deal of time to warm up this is recommended. If you do turn off your machine overnight (we prefer to do this), turn on the steam valves to expel all of the steam from the machine. This ensures that the internal parts of the machine are under no pressure overnight. Some newer machines have small pressure-release valves under the grill that let the machine de-pressurise slowly when it is off. The older ones don't though, so just in case your machine doesn't have this valve you should get into the habit of expelling all the steam once the machine has been turned off.

The Grinder

The grinder needs to be cleaned out at the end of each day. This is done to stop rancid oils building up in the hopper and so that the machine is nicely presented. We also like to do it to keep the beans fresh and to make sure that any ground coffee left over is not used the next day.

Wash the Hopper

Take the hopper off the grinder and store the beans in an airtight container in the cupboard. Wash the hopper in warm, soapy water then rinse it and let it air-dry. Washing removes the rancid oils that build up during the day from the beans. Do not put a wet hopper back on the grinder as moisture will find its way down the grinder and rust the blades.

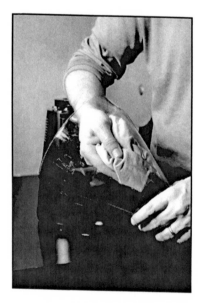

Empty the Chamber

You need to extract all the ground coffee that is in the chamber and store in an airtight container. Do not use this ground coffee again for hot espresso coffees the next day as freshness is compromised. We use this left-over ground coffee for Iced Coffees.

Take a small paint or pastry brush and ensure that all ground coffee has been evacuated from the chamber. We suggest that you run down the amount of coffee in the chamber towards the end of the day so that you do not end up storing masses of containers of ground coffee.

(Handy hint: close the gate half an hour before closing the café and let the grinder grind the beans that are left between the gate and the blades).

Final Buff

Clean down the outside of the grinder itself. Just use a buffing cloth and some window cleaner. We always want the grinder to look as clean as it did when we bought it.

Getting a Job in Coffee

Here are a few tips when going for a job in coffee:

Barista Courses
It is often best to do a barista course if you have had no experience. When deciding on a course make sure that the teachers are professional baristas with good experience. Make sure that the classes are small and that it is a hands-on course with half an espresso machine dedicated to you. In some courses you just listen to a 'teacher' talk for three hours and you get to make one cappuccino. This is a waste of time and money as what you want is some hands-on time with the espresso machine and grinder. Finally, make sure that the course covers the main points that we have in this book. Make sure that you get a nationally recognised and professional looking certificate that you can show potential employers.

Dress and Act like a Barista
Use the word 'barista' in your job application. If cold-calling on cafes, wear tidy clothing and ask to speak to the manager if he or she is not busy and submit your resume, highlighting the fact that you have completed a barista course if you have done one (highly recommended).

Talk to the Manager
Be wary of leaving your application with anyone other than a manager or owner as often resumés get 'lost' when not in the right hands (remember...nobody likes being replaced!). It is better to ask when the manager or owner is going to be in and come back then, rather than leaving your application in the wrong hands.

Make a Coffee for the Manager

If cold-calling on cafés and if talking to the manager/owner when the café is not busy, offer to make a trial coffee so that you can instantly impress with your skills.

Offer to do a Trial

In your application cover letter, offer to come in and fulfil a three hour unpaid 'trial' so that the manager/owner of the café can assess your barista and customer relations skills.

Keep Your Resume Simple

Ensure that your resumé is succinct but states your date of birth, full name, contact details including mobile phone number and e-mail address, education, availability and past work experience (whether or not connected to hospitality). One of our students actually got a graphic artist friend of hers to put some nice pictures of coffee cups on her one-page resumé. She got the first job she applied for. On the following pages we have a simple one-page resumé that you can follow.

Prepare a Cover Letter

If you are serious about getting a job enclose a cover letter with the name of the café and address it to the owner. A quick phone call will get you these details and it *is* worth it. On the following page you will see a sample cover letter.

EXAMPLE OF COVER LETTER
20th February, 2010

Jonathon Bravo
42 Artarmon Road, Artarmon, NSW, Australia 2064
Ph: (02) 9413 2459, Mobile: 0408 236 798, e-mail: john@optus.net

Joan's Café
448 Glebe Point Road
Glebe, NSW, 2037

Dear Mr. Thomas,

My name is Jonathon Bravo and I am interested in applying for any work you may have as a casual, working from anywhere between 10 and 25 hours per week. I am energetic, enthusiastic and I have a keen interest in coffee, after having recently completed a barista course (see attached certificate).

As well as understanding about customer service, cleanliness and efficiency, I am familiar with a coffee machine and know the different coffee styles that are demanded in a café environment. I can also clean the coffee machine and grinder and have an understanding of the importance of the coffee grind and I know how to adjust the espresso machine if it is not pouring espressos at or close to 30 seconds.

I would be willing to come in for a trial for a few hours on my own time so that you can put my skills to the test or alternatively, simply to come in at your convenience so that I can make a couple of coffees on the espresso machine with you watching on.

I don't know everything about coffee but I am a quick learner and as coffee is my passion, I am eager to find out as much as I can about perfecting the art of espresso.

Kind regards,
Jonathon Bravo

EXAMPLE OF RESUME

JONATHON BRAVO

Personal Details	42 Artarmon Road, Artarmon, 2064, N.S.W Ph: (02) 94132459 Mobile: 0408 236 798 e-mail: john@optus.net Date of Birth: 30/4/87
Employee Type	Casual (10-25 hrs per wk) Available every day except Tue/Wed & all evenings (N.B. I own my own car)

Education	* Maitland Public School (1992-1999)
	* Singleton High School (2000-2005)
	* UTS (Ultimo Campus) (2006-2009)
	  Bachelor of Business
	* Hunter Institute of TAFE (2009-2012)
	  Cert IV in Hospitality (correspondence)

Work Experience	* Sydney Catering Co. Feb 2006-Jan 2010 (Waiter/Food Preparation) * Mitre 10 Chatswood Dec 2006-Nov 2008 (casual sales assistant) * Bunnings Hardware Dec 2008-Nov 2009 (casual sales assistant)
Certificates Obtained	**SITHFAB012A Prepare and Serve Espresso Coffee & SITXOHS002A Follow Workplace Hygiene Procedures from** Barista Basics™ Coffee Academy, Sydney, NSW (Jan 2010)
References	Ms Sally Simpson, Sydney Catering Co. Ph: 9766 8766 Mr Tim Pope, Mitre 10 Chatswood Ph: 9766 5687 Mr Mark Lewis, Bunnings Hardware Ph: 9413 2876
Interests	Surfing, listening to music, eating out, watching films, indoor soccer

93

Keeping Your Job as a Barista

Some tips we would offer are:

Present Yourself Well
Ensure that you are always well presented. Wear clean clothes every day and adhere to the staff uniform regulations. You may not want to wear a uniform or wear a badge but if this is what is required don't bother questioning it. Regularly wash your apron.

Be Consistent
Try to implement the use of thermometers in your milk jugs when frothing milk if not already being done.

Take an active interest in the grind of the coffee and try to achieve the 30-second pour as you make coffees. Making the work of the barista more scientific will yield better coffees and make the job more interesting for you.

Clean, Clean and Clean Again
Try to implement daily back washing of the espresso machine and cleaning of grinder if not already being done.

Always clean the steam wand with a designated wipe cloth after each frothing session. Never allow milk to dry on it and if there is ever a build-up of milk on it during the day clean it off with a hot rag. Do not use steel wool.

Clean the coffee-making area regularly, including the jugs. Milk jugs with milk all over their exterior look unsightly and are unhygienic.

Make sure that all the cups and glasses are cleaned and stocked so that when it is busy there are enough on hand to cope with demand. Be sure to stack cups and glasses on the top of the espresso machine so that they are pre-warmed.

Finally, ensure you clean and polish the part of the espresso machine that faces your customers!

Personal Hygiene

It's true that being a barista is all about making good coffee. But you can't make good coffee if your personal hygiene isn't up to scratch.

We've seen some very basic personal hygiene rules that have gone by the wayside in some cafes we have been into.

As a starter, you can't be in the food service industry if you have bad dandruff. For goodness sake, go and buy some shampoo and conditioner that will rectify the problem.

Another basic rule that needs to be adhered to is hand washing at regular intervals. Local councils are cracking down on this during their inspections and rightly so. Cafés are now required to have a soap and towel dispenser near the sink, which should be very close to the coffee machine. Clean hands are essential as your hands are in constant contact with the top of the filter basket as you wipe off the coffee grinds before inserting the group handle into the group. Your hands are also coming into contact with the wipe cloth which is coming into contact with the steam wand which is inserted into the jug to froth the milk. It might sound like an indirect link between your hands and the milk but it is a link nonetheless.

Wearing clean clothes and clean aprons, using deodorant etc should all go without saying but far too often they are overlooked as people settle into their daily routine. Good baristas though, are on top of all of these aspects of personal hygiene.

Enough said.

Coffee Art

Do It!

Always try to improve your presentation by trying coffee art and varying the way you sprinkle chocolate on coffees. Customers love a nicely presented coffee and this is one major weapon against your competition. We developed the world's first coffee art course and we're so into it that we've just developed a very cool iPhone app featuring our coffee art. (See www.coffeeartapp.com)

Create Your Own

Always look for new ways to present your coffees. For example, you might want to try using chocolate fudge on top of your coffees if your café uses such fudge. The world is yours. Invent your own styles. The barista competitions always have one drink that you prepare yourself that is your own invention.

Free Pouring

One way to create impressive designs is to free pour the milk into the glass or cup in such a way that a milky, wave-like pattern is created that blends in with the crema.

To create a flower-like pattern begin pouring milk into the espresso towards the top of the glass. Pour gently into the crema in one spot. When the glass is about half filled, using a wrist action, shake the jug back and forth while slowly moving backward. A flower pattern will start to emerge and fill the top of glass. When the glass is just about full sweep the milk over the pattern to the other side of the glass. This will finish off the flower. Make sure that not too much milk comes out at the end as the pattern will sink.

Use Your Thermometer To Draw

We use our thermometers most of the time with our artwork. When pouring lattes we pour gently into the centre of the glass so that the crema is maintained. We then add some white creamy foam on top of the crema. We then simply drag white froth into the dark crema with the tip of our thermometer. Wipe after each time you do this. There are many designs that can be achieved with this method and your customers will love it.

It's all in the Pour

As the following illustrations show, latte art is simple once you have the grind right (nice crema) and your milk is silky (the thermometer glides through it). You can play off against the dark brown and white to create patterns easily.

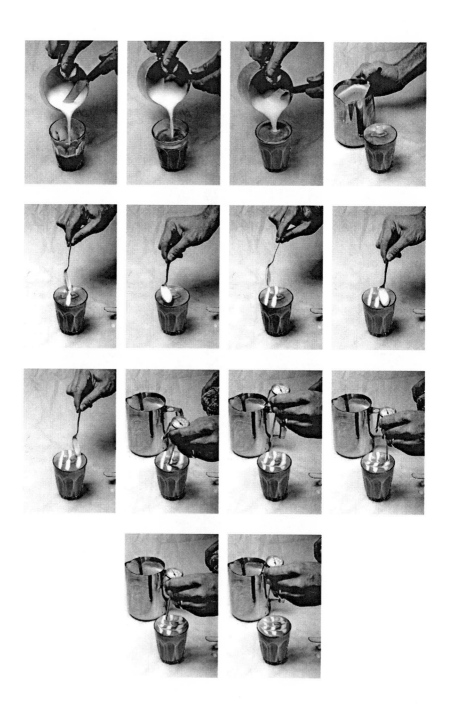

A Final Word on Being a Barista

Get on with the other Staff Members
When we hire we always look for people who can get on with our managers and other staff members. It is great to have an interest in the mating habits of stick insects in Borneo but if that is all you can discuss with your work mates (and even worse, customers!) you won't last long. Work in a café should be fun and interesting. You must make every effort to get on with everyone you work with. We try to hire staff with common interests.

Get to Know Your Customer
Getting to know your customer is the final step to being a great barista - and probably the most important. There is no doubt that with time you will perfect the cleaning of the espresso machine, the setting of the grinder, the frothing of the milk and the pouring of great coffees. Mastering the art of keeping and entertaining customers will take longer.

Some tips we have are as follows:

Get with the Rhythm
It is important to get a rhythm going in a busy café. You do not want to get flustered. In the best cafes the roles of each person are fully defined so that you minimise the time it takes to get a customer their coffee and also minimise mistakes. For example, if there are three people working, put one person on the cash register, one frothing and pouring milk and the third person should load the group handles, manage the flow of drinks and deliver them to customers.

Get to Know Your Customers' Names

In most cafes you will find that unless you are in a shopping mall or tourist area, about 80% of customers come in everyday. We challenge ourselves to learn four new names a day. The difference between remembering and not remembering names should not be underestimated. We all love to hear our own name - we feel special when it is remembered.

What are your Customers' Interests?

Once you know the customers' names find out more about them. Where do they work? What are their hobbies? Do they have kids? Do they play sport? Your customers come to you to get out of their world for a while. Most of them want to be entertained and want to feel that you are interested in them.

Keep Current

Turn on talk-back radio on the way to work and make sure you catch a news bulletin. A good barista will be able to discuss all things topical. If there is a big sports match on know who won or a little something about the game. You do not have to be interested or have watched it but you will still be able to discuss the match with those customers who are interested and are dying to tell you their point of view. If there are fireworks on that night in the city ask your customers if they are going.

Remember Your Customers' Orders

Everyone wants to be loved. We find that most customers order the same thing every day. In fact many come in and order that same drink at the same time every day. Just remembering what that order is proves to them that you love them and you are interested in them. In one of our cafes we used to make the coffees for customers as they crossed the road toward our café. As soon as they paid it was ready and they went away impressed at how much we cared about them. Sure we got it wrong occasionally as they headed into the post office next door and not our cafe - but you get the idea!

What Else Does Your Customer Want?

Make your customers feel at home when they come to see you. Constantly clean the tables and floor so that the customer has a clean space to enjoy their coffee. Also make sure they have everything they need to enjoy their stay. We had one customer who came in everyday at 4pm. He would only stay if we had a certain newspaper for him. So everyday at around 3:30pm we would set that paper aside for him. These are the little things that stop your customers from going next door.

Up-Selling

This is not an art. It just takes practice. For example, when your customer orders a latte, ask them if they want syrup with the latte. This simple question will increase your average sales that day. Just imagine if you then ask if they would like a cake with their order. Once again your average sales will increase. Often a customer will not think to order the syrup and may not know about your coffee and cake deal. Simple leading questions will certainly increase your sales.

(Handy hint: just don't be annoying).

The Home Barista and Domestic Bliss

Walking into the coffee machine section of your local department store these days is utterly confusing. So many prices, so many models, so many brands! We're even bombarded by advertisements that tell us that pretty soon the home espresso machine will be as indispensable as the hot water kettle, the fridge and the toaster! (Don't laugh – we actually think there is some element of truth to this.)

As we all know these days coffee is EVERYWHERE. People at work talk about it, people at the pub talk about it, people in the street talk about it. Everyone has an opinion. Everyone (pretty much) drinks it. As our tastes develop more and more people will want good coffee at home.

So isn't it time you threw out your instant coffee and drink at home what you drink at your local? (café, that is)

The Players
Sunbeam, Breville, Krups, Kitchenaid, Rancilio, Gaggia, De Longhi, Saeco, Giotto, Vibiemme, Jura, (amongst others).

The Prices
$70 - $4,000

The Quality of the Espresso
Excellent for most machines, even the very cheap ones.

The Quality of the Frothed Milk
On machines under $400, unfortunately not great. Given that 90% of coffee drinks consumed in places like Asia, Australia and the US are now milk-based, milk frothing is vitally important.

Minimum Spend
With domestic coffee machines, the old adage, "You get what you pay for" rings true.

If you want to make coffees for more than two people and not spend half an hour in the kitchen doing so, you need to spend at least $400 on a domestic machine. The reason is that most of the cheaper machines do not have large enough boilers to create enough steam to froth the milk. The milk is simply not able to 'swirl'. Without swirling you won't get that nice creamy texture that is the hallmark of a good gourmet coffee. Remember - frothy, aerated 'roadhouse' froth is *out*. Creamy, silky and shiny froth is *in*.

Machines above $800 can sometimes have twin boilers unlike the cheaper machines that operate on a heat exchange system. One boiler will heat the water for the espresso and a separate one will create the steam to froth the milk. This enables the user to extract espressos and froth milk at the same time.

We both have had $400 Saeco coffee machines at home (only because we inherited them as stock in some cafes we purchased) and they worked a treat. We have also had lots of experience on cheaper machines that family members own and that students bring in to get instruction on, and all of these cheaper machines fail in the milk department. To be brutally honest the consistency and texture of the milk is just not there.

If you have a 'small' machine though, do not despair. As mentioned above, the espresso you can get with these machines can be fantastic (with the correct grind, sometimes superior to what you can get on a $10,000 commercial machine!) and if you are only making coffee for one or two people, you can achieve moderately acceptable frothed milk.

The top-tier home machines are classified as 'semi commercial' machines. The best ones include Vibiemme and Giotto and are priced at around $3000. We both now own Vibiemmes at home and to be honest, don't know how we ever did without them. You do need to spend around $700 on a semi commercial grinder (we'd recommend a grind-on-demand system due to the sporadic use that a home machine gets....you don't want coffee sitting in a doser all day only to dispense stale coffee when you need your evening coffee!).

Using Your Home Espresso Machine
The following instructions are written in plain English (most instruction manuals aren't!) but as all machines are slightly different, please ensure that you study your machine's manual carefully before operating.

Before Using Each Day
1. Take out the water reservoir. Empty any old water and refill with fresh water. (Remember that nobody likes drinking mouldy or cockroach-infested water!)
2. Turn machine on and wait for the operating light to appear.

Modus Operandi
First make the espresso, then froth the milk. Remember that timing is everything with gourmet coffee.

Espresso
1. The rule is one scoop for one cup (using the single filter basket) and two scoops for two cups (using the double filter basket). If you don't have your own grinder at home, use

filter coffee purchased in a vacuum sealed 'brick pack' (not coffee ground for espresso – this type of coffee is only used in commercial espresso machines). Some brick packs these days specifically say they are a little finer than the traditional 'filter grind' coffee (which is best used for plungers). It is best to use these finer grinds with the home espresso machine as the water will take longer to travel through the ground coffee and into your cup, thereby extracting more flavour on its journey through the filter basket.

2. After filling the appropriate filter basket, insert the group handle (porta-filter) into the group and press the espresso button. Do this as soon as you can after the group handle is inserted as hot water from the group head itself may drip into the fresh coffee, causing bitterness if water is not infused directly afterwards.

3. The universally accepted amount of espresso for a standard coffee is 30ml (1 fl oz). In other words, it truly is a 'shot' just the same as you would order at your local bar. You may want to use a measuring cup to measure your first few espressos to gauge what 30ml looks like in your cup. You don't need to go out and buy an expensive measuring shot glass from your local catering outlet. Just go to a chemist and buy a plastic one made for measuring medicines. Make sure it can measure up to 50ml (1.75 fl oz) though so that there is room in the measuring cup after 30ml of espresso plus crema has been poured into it. At the end of the day though, of course if making for yourself, tasting is the best way to develop your own benchmark as to what level you should fill your cup with espresso.

4. Ensure that your espresso has a good crema. If not, your coffee grind may be at fault. As a rule of thumb, if the crema is too light or virtually non-existent and disappears quickly, the grind is too coarse (water from the machine has passed too quickly through the compacted coffee, thereby not extracting enough flavour from the coffee). Alternatively if the crema is too dark, inconsistent and bubbly, the grind is too fine (water from the machine has passed too slowly through the compacted coffee, thereby extracting too many bad elements from the coffee. The espresso will smell burnt and will taste very bitter). The right grind sits somewhere in between and results in a nice, consistent, honeycomb-coloured, oily layer that hides all of the jet-black espresso below it. It will not disappear quickly, but will 'hold' on top for quite some time. Good crema = tasty coffee.

Milk (see Chapter 7 for pictures on milk frothing)

(Handy hint: some machines come with an external sheath or 'froth enhancer' that sits over the steam wand – this can be stripped off and thrown away as it will produce 'roadhouse' froth).

1. Switch the steaming button on the espresso machine to the 'on' position and open the steam valve. Ensure that you have a cloth underneath the wand to catch the first bit of water that will come through before the steam. You do this to ensure that you are only getting steam in your milk jug, not water.

2. Now immerse your 600ml (21 fl oz) stainless steel jug (which you should fill to just underneath the spout) under the steam wand and open the valve.

3. Try to establish a circular swirling motion of the milk in the jug. We always find that this can be achieved easily by having a right angle between the handle of the jug and the steam wand and having the steam wand touching the side of the jug.

4. Lower the jug down gently until the bottom of the steam wand is just touching the top of the milk. You should hear a hissing/bubbling sound. This is the correct position for froth to be formed. To maintain this sound (and hence the frothing) you will need to keep lowering the jug, millimetre by millimetre, as the froth naturally rises in the jug. Be careful not to lose the circular motion. Only move the jug in the up/down plane, do not move it from side to side. Avoid moving the jug up and down as you heat the milk. The only direction you should be going at this stage is down.

5. When you are happy with the amount of froth or when the jug starts to get pretty hot, stop lowering the jug. You may even want to lift the jug up to heat and texture the bottom layer of the milk. Remember - do not lose the circular motion.

6. Turn off the steam wand after the milk has reached about 65°C/150°F (the jug will feel incredibly hot to touch).

7. Pour as soon as you have finished (after expelling any air bubbles by 'banging' the jug on the counter). You should have no large bubbles, only lots of tiny bubbles, on the surface of the milk. The milk should be creamy, silky and shiny in appearance.

8. Pour the milk into the espresso but try to pour in one spot only, letting the crema 'rise' in the cup. Nice creamy milk can be added at the end where latte art can now be attempted.

Regular Cleaning

1. Turn off the machine and let it cool. Open up the steam valve and de-pressurise the machine.

* Steam wand

>   Unscrew the steam head mechanism and dismantle it, cleaning with warm, soapy water.

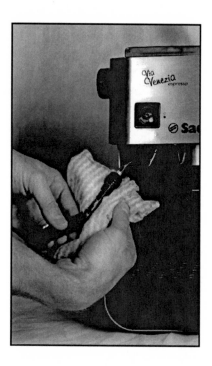

>   Clean the nozzle hole with a pin or paper clip. Reassemble the steam head mechanism and screw it back onto the steam wand. Wipe the whole steam wand with a cloth.

* Group Handle (Porta-Filter)
- Remove from group and take out filter basket, tipping out the spent coffee (not into the sink but in the rubbish bin, or better still on the garden!) and thoroughly wash with steel wool to remove any rancid coffee oil. Soak the group handle and clean the metallic part. Allow to dry.

- Take a small-handled screwdriver and remove the shower screen from the group and clean with steel wool.

All holes in the shower screen should be completely unblocked when finished.

Wipe up in the inside of the group thoroughly before reinserting the shower screen. At this time, the clean group handle can be reinserted into the machine.

* Exterior of the Machine

Wipe down with a warm cloth to remove any spilt milk/coffee. If feeling energetic you may even polish with a polishing cloth and stainless steel cleaner or window cleaner!

Periodic Cleaning
Descaling

The formation of lime and calcium build-up may result over time as your machine is used. Descaling can remove this build-up.

1. Mix the descaling solution with the water in the reservoir. (Contact the distributor of your machine to establish where you can buy this solution). A triple action cleaner works wonders at removing sediment and oil build-up as well.

2. Remove the shower screen by unscrewing it.

3. Press the espresso button to allow the diluted descaling solution to flow through the group, cup by cup. After every cup allow about 10-15 minutes for the solution to take effect by turning off the machine using the main switch. Resume by turning on the machine and following the above instructions.

4. Rinse the water reservoir thoroughly upon completion of the above process and refill with fresh water. Allow about 2/3 of the fresh water to rinse through the system by pressing the espresso button again. This will expel all the diluted descaling solution from the inner workings of the machine.

5. Tip out the remaining water in the reservoir.

6. Reinsert the shower screen by screwing it back on.

(Handy hint: do not use vinegar to clean your machine).

Storing Your Coffee

We recommend using an *airtight* container stored in a dark, cool place. It is not necessary to store your coffee in the freezer or fridge (coffee takes in aromas from food and also water molecules, causing it to lose freshness prematurely).

If you have a coffee grinder we recommend that you grind only enough coffee for your present use as coffee begins to go stale once it is ground if not stored correctly.

Choosing a Coffee Company

Begin with the Bean

The great thing about living in a capitalist society is that when there is a competitive market out there the consumer is always king. That's pretty much the way it is with coffee and it is becoming increasingly so.

When you are in the market for coffee for the first time or when thinking of switching from your current supplier, always begin by asking about the *bean*. You see, it's all about the bean. Don't get carried away by umbrellas, windbreaks and free ceramic cups - you must focus on the coffee as this is what will bring customers back.

Pertinent questions might be:

[1] Is your coffee roasted locally? (Remember that beans that have been shipped out from overseas will not be fresh as if they have been roasted locally.)

[2] How often is it roasted? (Good roasters will be roasting all week.)

[3] Is it a blend and if so, what beans are in the blend? (Complex blends are good, especially with African, South American, Indian and Papua New Guinean beans.)

[4] Is there any robusta in it? (Remember that small amounts of high-grade robusta are fine. Just don't buy coffee that has a huge amount of robusta in it.)

[5] How often would you deliver the coffee? (You should be getting the coffee at least once fortnightly or preferably once per week.)

[6] Does your 1kg (2.2lbs) bag have a one-way valve in it to ensure that oxygen can't get in? (Bags with valves are preferable.)

[7] Are there different roasts that we can try? (You may prefer a lighter or darker roast to the one most other cafés receive.)

[8] How much per kilo is the coffee and what are the payment terms? (You shouldn't be paying more than $25-$30 per kilo in today's market.)

[9] Can someone from the coffee company come in and set up the grinder so that it dispenses 7g (0.25oz) per throw and check the initial grind setting to illustrate to the staff what the perfect espresso should look like? (If they can't, don't go with them as this working knowledge and willingness to get you started is going to be indicative of your ongoing support.)

[10] Do you sell any retail packs so that our customers can take home the coffee they enjoy in our establishment? (Attractive 114g/250g (4oz/8.8oz) vacuum-sealed 'brick packs' are great sellers, as are 500g (1.1lbs) bags of beans.) Can you supply a couple of small perspex stands explaining the blends with pricing attached?

[11] How many other cafés in the immediate area take your coffee? (You can probably find this out for yourself by walking around the block. Being a little bit different from your competitors always helps.)

Other Issues to Ponder

Of course there are other issues that will help sway the decision of whether to go with one coffee company over another. Introducing some branding into your establishment is sometimes a good way to go. We're talking here about branded sugar sticks, branded serviettes and branded take-away cups (don't go for foam, ensure the cups are paper or the new style ripple cups). You will have to pay for these, and yes, they are slightly more expensive than their generic counterparts, but the margin that you are making per cup of coffee will well and truly cover these small costs.

Other products you may share in the cost of with your coffee company include aprons, staff shirts, name badges, ceramic cups (ensure they have 12oz, 8oz and espresso cups with saucers), wind barriers, umbrellas, latte glasses, light boxes, static clings for your front window, display boxes for your retail packs, etc.

Grinders and Coffee Machines

As café owners and barista trainers, we have always owned our own equipment so that we can maintain our independence and achieve the lowest price possible from the coffee company. It doesn't take a genius to work out that if you are getting your coffee company to put machines in on loan, you will be paying for it, if not through rental instalments, then through an increased cost of your coffee. If your coffee company puts in a machine on loan, you will probably have to sign a contract for a period of time tying you to buying a set amount of kilos at a set price.

Having said this however, most good coffee companies will supply machines willingly, but you will have to be using a good amount of kilos per week to make it worthwhile for them (say more than 10kg = 22lbs).

Grinders are another story altogether. Most coffee companies should be able to supply these on loan at no cost to you, even if you are not using 10kg per week. The main reason that these are supplied more readily is that it is going to be better for the coffee company to be supplying beans rather than ground coffee for freshness reasons and because the café really needs to be adjusting their grind daily, rather than getting a predetermined one from the coffee company. The coffee will taste better, you will sell more cups and in turn buy more beans from the coffee company.

Break the Stereotype

A reasonable percentage of city café owners have, over the last five or so years, developed a certain arrogance which particularly manifests itself when they deal with coffee companies.

You can be the big man on campus in front of your staff and pester the coffee company for freebies galore, but it doesn't mean that you will get the best service. This may sound unbelievable, but we have known some coffee companies to simply stop supplying certain customers when they become too problematic, so it is worth keeping this in mind. Cafés that switch suppliers every six months end up with a very confused clientele.

Having been on both sides of the fence ourselves, we find that being pleasant and not overly demanding will strengthen your relationship with your coffee company and you will end up with better service.

Just remember that the relationship has to be a two-way street for everyone to benefit.

References

Davids, K. (2001) *Coffee: A Guide to Buying, Brewing and Enjoying.* New York: St Martin's Griffin

Davids, K. (1993) *Espresso: Ultimate Coffee.* California: 101 Productions/Cole Group

Arvidson, E. & Milletto, B. (1997) *Bean Business Basics.* Bellissimo: Oregon.

Internet: www.cafedirect.co.uk, www.nzcoffee.co.uk, www.lucidcafe.com, www.caffenero.com, www.koffeekorner.com, www.coffeeuniverse.com, www.coffeeresearch.org, www.virtualcoffee.com.

Barista Courses

To book into the Barista Basics™ Coffee Academy, you can either book online at www.baristabasics.com.au, call us on 1300 366 218 or cut out and fax this form back to us on (02) 9966 8841.

Full name for certificate:

Mobile phone contact number:

Credit card #:

Name on credit card:

Expiry date on credit card:

Preferred date of course:

E-mail address:

Previous Experience: Yes / No (if yes, please state what experience you have had)

[this page intentionally blank]

DVD Purchases

To buy *The Coffee Menu* and/or *Master Barista* and/or *Coffee Art and Presentation Techniques* visit www.baristabasics.com.au, call us on 1300 366 218 or alternatively cut out and fax this form back to us on (02) 9235 2434. Please note that there is an additional charge of $10 for postage within Australia.

Orders are processed and sent within 3 business days of this form being faxed to the above number.

Name of DVD title requested:

Credit card #:

Name on credit card:

Expiry date on credit card:

Total amount to be charged to credit card:

Address for postage (within Australia):

Mobile phone contact number:

E-mail address for confirmation of postage to be sent to:

For online orders within Australia please see www.baristabasics.com.au and for international orders visit www.baristabasics.com

[this page intentionally blank]

Barista Accessories Purchases

(pictures on next page)

To purchase our barista accessories visit www.baristabasics.com.au, call us on 1300 366 218 or alternatively cut out and fax this form back to us on (02) 9235 2434. Please note that there is an additional charge of $10 for postage within Australia.

Orders are processed and sent within 3 business days of this form being faxed to the above number.

Name of barista accessory requested:

Credit card #:

Name on credit card:

Expiry date on credit card:

Total amount to be charged to credit card:

Address for postage (within Australia):

Mobile phone contact number:

E-mail address for confirmation of postage to be sent to:

For online orders within Australia please see www.baristabasics.com.au and for international orders visit www.baristabasics.com

Tampers – 58mm and 52mm
(commercial) (domestic)

Thermometers

Spatulas

Timers

Stencils

Acknowledgements

Our sincere thanks to Melva Gee, Vanessa Leong, Caryl Lightfoot and Alice Eddowes for their time in editing this book.

Thanks also must go to Barry Heffernan from Knockrow Ridge Coffee whose time in explaining how his coffee is grown, processed and roasted was invaluable in the compilation of this book. His coffee is amongst the best we have tasted and we would encourage anyone travelling north on the Pacific Highway from Ballina to Brisbane to stop off and buy some of his beans. We'd also recommend Red Door Coffee in the same region for those wanting a great coffee bean roasted to perfection.

Thanks also to our chief photographers, George Murray and Joanna Gee.

Finally, thanks to Enzo Massarotti and Salvatore Savarino for their advice and insight into coffee over the years.

David Gee and Matthew Gee are experienced café owners and coffee wholesalers. They are widely regarded in the coffee industry as Australia's leading barista trainers.

They also run one of the most highly regarded Barista courses in Australia. With their courses, the point of difference in the marketplace is their focus on smaller class sizes and multiple teachers. Every student gets hands-on experience with their own part of the machine, including a steam wand.

At the conclusion of each course graduating students are awarded with a Barista certificate as well as a nationally recognised RTO certificate bearing the qualifications SITHFAB012A Prepare and Serve Espresso Coffee and SITXOHS002A Follow Workplace Hygiene Procedures as well as a wealth of online course materials. Job referrals as well as general information about the industry can also be obtained.

For more information on their courses as well as their Café Management classes, visit their website **www.baristabasics.com.au** or **www.baristabasics.com** or call them directly on ph: 1300 366 218 (international +612 8081 2515). Also visit their blog on www.baristabrothers.com for all things coffee and their app site www.coffeeartapp.com.

Courses are run almost every day of the week in Sydney, Melbourne and Brisbane. As classes are limited, bookings are essential.

CPSIA information can be obtained at www.ICGtesting.com
Printed in the USA
LVOW131648250213

321618LV00007B/994/P